To

From

Date

Mini Devotions for Girls

an imprint of Christian Art Publishers,
PO Box 1599, Vereeniging, 1930, RSA

First edition 2019

Devotions taken from *One-Minute Devotions® for Girls*

Cover designed by Christian Art Kids

Designed by Christian Art Kids

Images used under license from Shutterstock.com

Printed in China

ISBN 978-1-4321-3140-1

21 22 23 24 25 26 27 28 29 30 – 13 12 11 10 9 8 7 6 5 4

Printed in Shenzhen, China
MAY 2021
Print Run: 110238

MINI DEVOTIONS

for Girls

CAROLYN LARSEN

christian art kids

The Beginning

1

In the beginning God created
the heavens and the earth.

Genesis 1:1

Everything began with God. Before He started creating, there wasn't any earth, sky, people, animals – nothing.

Look around you at the world He made. Think about the ocean, mountains, wind, rain, lightning, butterflies, elephants, your mind, your heart ... what a powerful God. Not just powerful either, He pays attention to detail.

He knows the biggest things in the world and the smallest. He made you. He loves you. He has a plan for your life. He's worth getting to know. The Bible is His story and by reading it you will learn how He has taken care of His people and how He will take care of you and love you more than you can even imagine.

Dear God, when I stop and think about Your power and Your creativity, I'm blown away that You care about me. It's amazing ... and I'm so thankful that You do. Amen.

2

The Human Mold

Then God said, "Let us make man
in Our image, in Our likeness."

Genesis 1:26

Okay, you have bad days, weeks, months. You may even sometimes feel like you are just one big mess with no reason for being or purpose on earth.

Well, these ten words spoken by God prove that isn't true. You are made in God's image. Think about that for a minute. He is wisdom, love, power, creativity ... anything you can think of is possible in you because all of it was made *by* God and *is* God.

All of that was put into Adam and Eve – your ancestors. God made you and He gave you unique abilities and talents – just like Him! Cool, huh?

Dear God, sometimes I feel so useless and dumb. When I start feeling that way, remind me that I'm made in Your image and that means I'm worth something! You didn't make any garbage! Amen.

No Foolin'

3

The LORD God banished him from the Garden of Eden to work the ground from which he had been taken.

Genesis 3:23

Have you ever tried to get away with something? Come on, be straight – your mom or dad tells you, "Do this" or "Don't do that" but you do exactly what you're not supposed to do. Then you try to lie your way out of it or blame someone else ... anything to avoid punishment.

Adam and Eve tried that after breaking the one rule God gave them. It didn't work, though. God knew what they had done and He punished them for it.

God doesn't take disobedience. He punishes it. He sent Adam and Eve out of the Garden of Eden. Don't ever think you can fool God. Because you can't.

Dear God, I know there isn't any chance at all of fooling You. Well, the truth is that I don't want to fool You. Please help me be honest with You all the time. Amen.

Count on It

I have set My rainbow in the clouds, and it will be the sign of the covenant between Me and the earth.

Genesis 9:13

Promises. They are great if they are kept. But if you have ever been the victim of a broken promise, you know how much it hurts and how hard it is to trust the promise-maker the next time.

If you've ever been the promise-breaker you have probably learned that your friends don't trust you so readily the next time.

God makes promises. This one from Genesis is the one He made with mankind through Noah. The rainbow is the sign of this promise. One thing you can count on with God – He keeps His promises ... always. Count on it.

Dear God, sometimes I start to feel about You the way I feel about people. Then I wonder if I can trust You – if You will always keep Your word. Thanks for this reminder that You mean what You say ... I can count on it. Amen.

Never Alone

5

God said, "I will be with you."

Exodus 3:12

Those are five pretty powerful words, aren't they? God said them to Moses, right after He gave Moses a job to do. Moses was scared that he couldn't handle the job, but God reminded him that he wasn't alone.

God's Word is filled with that same promise to you ... God will be with you. Whatever life brings, whatever job God gives you to do, you don't have to handle it alone.

That's comforting when you feel you aren't up to the job, or that you don't have the brains or strength or creativity to do the job before you.

God didn't just toss you into this world and say, "You're on your own!" Nope, He's with you every step of the way, giving guidance, strength ... whatever you need. He promised!

Dear God, thanks. I'm glad that You are always with me. I don't know what I'd do without You. Amen.

6

Miracle Worker

The Israelites went through the sea on dry ground with a wall of water on their right and on their left.

Exodus 14:22

More tension than any movie or TV show – God frees the Israelites from slavery and Egypt, and Moses leads them into the wilderness. Then the Egyptian king decides he wants them back and sends his whole army after them.

So, the Israelites are stuck with the Red Sea behind them and the Egyptian army in front of them ... hopeless?

Not when God is on your side. He parted the waters and they walked right through. God can do whatever He needs to do to protect you, help you, guide you.

Pay attention to your life every day and you just might see God commanding the unusual on your behalf!

Dear God, wow! I'm going to keep my eyes open every day to see what You might do to take care of me! Amen.

Big and Little

The LORD said to Moses, "I will rain down bread from heaven for you."

Exodus 16:4

Do you sometimes wonder if God really cares about the little things that worry you? Does He only care about the big spiritual things or do things like whether or not you have food, friends, what sports you play, how you treat others, or topics for papers you must write mean anything to Him? He cares about everything.

Look what He did for the Israelites. They were wandering around in the wilderness and they ran out of food. They got hungrier and hungrier so He rained down bread from heaven for them.

God took care of their immediate need and He will do the same for you. Tell Him what you need today.

Dear God, it's amazing that You care about the things that I worry about – even the little things. Thank You for caring and for helping. Amen.

8

Out of the Mouth ...

God spoke all these words: "I am the Lord your God, who brought you out of Egypt, out of the land of slavery."

Exodus 20:1-2

Maybe you're wondering what those words have to do with you. After all, God didn't bring you out of Egypt or free you from slavery.

Well, these are the words God spoke as He began writing the Ten Commandments on tablets of stone. Yeah, you're probably paying more attention now, aren't you?

The Ten Commandments are God's guidelines for how we should treat one another and God. If everyone would just live by these simple guidelines the world would be a much happier place. Give it a try. Read Exodus 20 and see how you match up with obeying the Ten Commandments.

Dear God, sometimes I think I'm doing pretty good, but when I honestly look at the Ten Commandments and how I obey them ... I kind of stink. Help me to live by them. I know I'd be happier and so would everyone around me. Amen.

Reminders

"Be strong and courageous. Do not be terrified; do not be discouraged, for the LORD your God will be with you wherever you go."

Joshua 1:9

The Israelites had followed Moses for a long time through some tough things. But, now he was dead and Joshua was in charge. Why should the people listen to him? Why should they do anything he said? He could have been shaking in his boots – except for these few words from God.

About three times in the first chapter of Joshua God told the new leader to be strong and courageous. He had nothing to be afraid of – God was with him.

The same thing holds true for you – if other kids give you a hard time, if unbelieving family members push you around – don't be afraid. No matter what you face, you're not alone. God is with you wherever you go!

Dear God, keep reminding me that I'm not alone. Sometimes life is hard and I don't think I can make it by myself. It's good to know that I don't have to. Amen.

Shower-time

Consecrate yourselves, for tomorrow
the LORD will do amazing things among you.

Joshua 3:5

Imagine taking a nice hot shower using your favorite sweet-smelling shower gel and bodybuilding shampoo. Feels good, right? After the shower you dry with a nasty sour-smelling towel and put on dirty stinky clothes. That just made the shower a waste of time, didn't it? That kind of describes what Joshua was telling his people in this verse.

Clean yourselves up, confess your sin, turn away from it, humble yourselves before God ... and stay clean. He said they would then see God do amazing things for them.

Do you want God to do amazing things in your life? Well, your heart and life clean up must come first ... get busy ... then you will see God do amazing things!

Dear God, I want to see You do amazing things in my life. Help me. Show me how to clean up my life and help me learn to humble myself before You. Amen.

Second Chances

"O Sovereign LORD, remember me.
O God, please strengthen me just once more."

Judges 16:28

Do you know who spoke these words? Samson – the strongest man who ever lived. God blessed Samson with incredible strength; as long as he lived by the rules God gave him.

Of course, Samson broke the rules and was captured by his enemies. But Samson learned a lesson. He recognized that his strength and power didn't come from his muscles or his good looks – it came from God. So, he asked for another chance and God gave it to him. He helped Samson, blind and in chains, defeat his powerful enemies.

God loves you and wants you to succeed in life. Keep asking for His help and live the way He tells you to live. Keep asking.

Dear God, I mess up so often. I'm sorry. I'm so sorry. Please forgive me and give me another chance. Amen.

Good Ears

"I have looked upon My people
for their cry has reached Me."

1 Samuel 9:16

Sometimes it feels like your prayers don't get past the ceiling, right? Not so, my friend. He hears.

God spoke these words just before He gave the Israelites the king they had been begging for. He heard their prayers and responded. God always hears. Sometimes He answers right away with a resounding "yes." Sometimes He takes His time and gives you a chance to discover whether that prayer is really something you want. Sometimes He protects you from your own foolishness and simply says, "No."

Whatever His answer, be sure of this – your prayers do not fall on deaf ears or an uncaring heart.

Dear God, thank You for hearing my prayers. Thank You for caring about the things that are on my mind and heart. Amen.

David and Goliath

"You come against me with sword and spear and javelin, but I come against you in the name of the LORD Almighty, the God of the armies of Israel, whom you have defied."

1 Samuel 17:45

David and Goliath. The classic story of big battling little and little coming out on top. The story of David and Goliath from the world's point of view finds no reason David should win. Goliath was bigger, stronger, had more experience. He had armor and a shield and spear. David had ... a sling and stones. But David knew that he had God on his side and no sword, spear or javelin had a chance against Him.

So, what does this mean to you? Plain talk – what tough things are you facing? From family problems to your own self-esteem ... come to the battle in the name of the Lord Almighty. Nothing can stand against that!

Dear God, thanks for being on my side. I want to always live and fight in Your name. Help me stay close to You. Amen.

Wise Choices

So God said to him, "Since you have asked for this ... I will give you a wise and discerning heart, so that there will never have been anyone like you, nor will there ever be."

1 Kings 3:11-12

If you could have anything in the world, what would you want? Think a minute before you answer. Would you ask for fame? Wealth? Would you want that creep in homeroom to be covered with pimples? God told King Solomon to ask for anything he wanted. Solomon wanted to be a good leader for his people so he asked God to make him wise.

God was pleased with his choice so He made him wise ... and rich beyond Solomon's wildest dreams. God honors wise choices. If you're asking God to bless your decisions and the choices you make, think of others before yourself.

Dear God, I don't mean to always think about myself first. Help me to think about others and to do things that will help them. Amen.

Never Too Young

15

Who knows but that you have come
to royal position for such a time as this.

Esther 4:14

Hey – I'm just a kid. I want to have fun. I'll think about important stuff when I'm older. Sound familiar? Esther wasn't very old. She was a young Jewish girl who won a beauty contest and became queen. But she was reminded that she might have become queen so God could use her to save the Jewish people in her land from being murdered.

Esther had to be courageous (she could have been killed, too). She had to be honest (the king didn't know she was Jewish). She had to trust God to take care of her and she asked others to pray for her. God can use you, too. Can you be courageous, honest, and trust Him? Sure you can … and don't forget to ask others to hold you up in prayer.

Dear God, I can't imagine doing something important like Esther. Help me to be courageous, honest and to trust You. Amen.

Delighted!

Blessed is the man who does not walk in the counsel of the wicked or stand in the way of sinners or sit in the seat of mockers. But his delight is in the law of the LORD.

Psalm 1:1-2

Who matters more to you than anything? Do you try to be just like your friends? Dress like them? Have the same opinions? Like the same things? Even if you sometimes know that the things they do or think are wrong?

What delights you? That's a word you probably don't use too often. "I'm delighted to hang out at the mall with you guys!" Nah – it doesn't sound right. Stop and think about it, though.

When something delights you, it brings you pleasure. What does that for you? Is it being just like your friends or is it pleasing God? Do you find delight in His Word and learning how He wants you to live? I hope so ... that delights Him!

Dear God, my friends are really important to me. But I don't want them to be more important than You. Help me delight in Your Word. Amen.

Smarts

The fear of the LORD is the beginning of knowledge,
but fools despise wisdom and discipline.

Proverbs 1:7

Think you're pretty smart, do ya? Do you even sometimes brag that you aren't scared of *anything*? Well, even if you believe that's true, it may not be a good thing.

Fear of the Lord is where smarts begins. Now this doesn't mean so much fear, like fear of the dark or fear of spiders. It means a healthy full-blooded *respect*. When you begin to understand God's power and that He absolutely will not tolerate sin, especially deliberate sin, then you begin to respect who He is.

That's when your knowledge begins. Part of that respect is understanding that God will discipline you sometimes, just as your parents do. He cares about you and wants you to learn and grow in your faith.

Dear Father, help me to be smart. Help me learn to respect You and to learn and grow. Thanks for caring. Amen.

Plan of Love

For to us a child is born, to us a son is given,
and the government will be on His shoulders.
And He will be called Wonderful Counselor,
Mighty God, Everlasting Father, Prince of Peace.

Isaiah 9:6

A plan. That's what God has had since the beginning of time. Nothing – not one thing – has happened that has surprised Him. He has probably been disappointed a few times, but not surprised. He knew the choice Adam and Eve would make. He knew every time that the Israelites would complain about stuff.

He knows when you're going to choose to turn away from Him rather than obey Him. He knows … and He loves you anyway. In fact, He loved mankind so much that He sent His Son to teach people how to live. Then He died and rose back to life so that anyone who believes in Him can one day go to heaven. That's quite a plan. A plan based on love.

Dear Lord, thank You that from the very beginning You have had a loving plan for mankind and for me. Amen.

Stuck like glue

You will keep in perfect peace him whose mind is steadfast, because he trusts in You.

Isaiah 26:3

What image pops into your mind when you think about peace? A quiet lake reflecting the mountains around it? A dove silently flying across the sky? A baby quietly sleeping? Is your life quiet and peaceful like that? Do you want it to be? How do you get it?

This little verse in Isaiah has the answer – keep your mind and heart on God. Don't just think about Him once in a while, settle your mind into a pattern of thinking about Him. Keep your mind stuck on Him – like glue. The more you think about Him, read His Word, talk to Him, the better you will know Him and the more you will trust Him.

So, there you go – sticking like glue to God leads to trusting Him which leads to peace. Simple.

Dear God, I want peace in my life. Please help me to learn to settle my mind on You. Help me learn to trust You so I can find real peace. Amen.

Fiery Faith

Praise be to the God of Shadrach,
Meshach and Abednego, who has sent
His angel and rescued His servants!

Daniel 3:28

"Throw out your faith in God or be thrown into a white hot fire!" There's no halfway ... there is only *no God* or *fire*! Shadrach, Meshach and Abednego had to make that choice and they chose God. Each of those young men loved God so much that they were ready to die for their faith.

Amazing ... do you love *anything* enough that you would be willing to die for it? Well, God honored their faith. He protected them in the fiery furnace – no, He didn't just protect them, He sent His angel to walk in the fire with them! The king who threw them in there in the first place was so impressed that he began praising God. God honors faith. Lives are changed by active faith.

Dear God, those guys were brave! Help me to learn to have that kind of faith. I love You now. I want to love You more! Amen.

Fish Story

The LORD provided a great fish to swallow Jonah, and Jonah was inside the fish three days and three nights.

Jonah 1:17

So ... how about the whole "obeying" thing? Does it seem like there is *always* someone telling you what to do? When the things you're told to do are things you *do not* want to do, then it's even stinkier! Jonah knew about that. God told him to warn the people in Nineveh to clean up their act.

Jonah didn't want to. He didn't even like the Ninevites! So, he took off in the opposite direction. Apparently he thought God wouldn't know where he was. *Wrong.*

The bottom line is that Jonah ended up in the belly of a fish for three days and nights to think about disobeying. He decided it was better to obey and God gave him another chance when the fish kind of, umm, threw him up. So ... obey God. It's the best choice.

Dear God, obeying is hard. Help me to remember that it's important to obey ... especially You. Amen.

Singular

"No one can serve two masters. Either he will hate the one and love the other, or he will be devoted to the one and despise the other. You cannot serve both God and money."

Matthew 6:24

Fill a glass to the top with water. Can you fill that same glass with milk? Of course not, it's already full of water. It can't be filled with two things.

Your heart can't be full of two things either. When there are two things shouting for your attention and energy, you will end up resenting one of them. Some people pour love for money into their hearts instead of love for God.

Money can't be the most important thing in your life. God wants to be most important and He will not share the number one spot with anything else. Be devoted to God alone.

Dear God, it's so tempting to want more and more money. But I don't want anything to be more important to me than You are. Help me to be filled with You and You alone. Amen.

Good Gifts

"If you, then, though you are evil, know how to give good gifts to your children, how much more will your Father in heaven give good gifts to those who ask Him."

Matthew 7:11

God wants to give you good things. Think about that ... the Creator of the universe *wants* to give you good things. Even more than your own mom and dad want to give you stuff. He loves you that much.

"Well, okay," you say. " Bring it on, God. Give me all you want!" Hold on there – what God wants to give you may not be "stuff" like MP3 players or designer clothes.

He wants to give you things that will grow your faith in Him and your sensitivity to other people. He wants to make you a better person. He cares that much!

Dear God, it blows me away that You love me that much! Thank You for every gift You have already given me. Help me to become the woman You want me to be. Amen.

Real Love

"For God so loved the world that He gave His one and only Son, that whoever believes in Him shall not perish but have eternal life."

John 3:16

It may not feel like it sometimes, but your parents love you – a lot! Most parents would do anything to protect their children from any kind of pain. The average mom or dad would never set their child up to be hurt at all.

But, God did. He had one Son ... one. No other kids at home to help ease the pain. He sent His one Son, Jesus, away from home (heaven) to live on earth. He taught people how to treat each other and how to worship God. Some of them responded by torturing Him and killing Him and God let it happen ... because of His love for those very people.

You are a part of those people. God did it for mankind. He loves us that much.

Dear God, it must have hurt You to see what Jesus went through. Thank You for loving me that much. Amen.

Bread and Water

25

"I am the bread of life. He who comes to Me will never go hungry, and he who believes in Me will never be thirsty."

John 6:35

Bread and water are not exactly gourmet foods. But bread and water are staples of a good diet. A person can live for a long time on bread and water. Jesus promised to be bread and water for His children.

In this verse, He isn't saying that your stomach will never growl or you will never have a cotton mouth. He is saying that your soul will never be hungry or thirsty again if you come to Him. He is all you need.

Jesus will fill you with His love. He will care for you and protect you. He will guide you and teach you. You need nothing else but Him.

Dear God, this is so hard to understand 'cause it seems like there are so many things that I need. Help me to understand how Jesus can be everything to me. I want to learn that. Amen.

Never Alone

"I will ask the Father and He will give you another Counselor to be with you forever – the Spirit of truth."

John 14:16-17

Saying goodbye stinks! Have you ever had to say goodbye to a friend who moved away? What about a broken-hearted goodbye to a boyfriend? A real heart-wrenching goodbye is never easy!

Jesus knew He was going to die. He knew His time on earth was finished and He knew that His leaving was not going to be easy for His friends. After all, He had spent pretty much every minute for 3½ years with them. They would miss Him.

So He asked His Father to send someone to be with them. That was the Holy Spirit. Jesus cared about His friends so much that He didn't want them to be alone. He wanted them to always know His presence and to keep learning and growing in their faith.

Dear Father, thank You that Jesus cared so much. Thank You that You care that much, too. I know the Holy Spirit is always with me. Amen.

Copycat

Be imitators of God, therefore, as dearly loved children, and live a life of love.

Ephesians 5:1-2

Okay, be honest. Do you and your friends buy the same style and brand of clothes? Do you like the same music? Do you like to do the same things? Seriously ... aren't you kind of imitators of whatever style is really hot right now?

Jesus gave a standard to copy. He said everyone should imitate God – be a copycat of God. He even explained what that means. Imitating God means loving other people. A life of love means loving – not just when you feel like it.

Loving your friends who are a lot like you, now that's easy. A life of love means loving those who are different from you. It means loving when it isn't easy. To love like that, you have to be close to God – you must copy Him!

Dear Father, help me to learn to love like that. It isn't easy to love kids who are different from me and my friends. Help me love like You do. Amen.

Love Hurts

The Lord disciplines those He loves.

Hebrews 12:6

Discipline ... is not fun. Being grounded or punished by having privileges taken away stinks. Did you ever think about the fact that your parents don't enjoy punishing you? The old saying, "This hurts me more than it hurts you," is actually true. However, discipline is necessary.

It keeps you from continually doing wrong things. Parents have to discipline you, but it makes them sad to make you sad.

God's discipline is very similar. He disciplines you because He loves you. But He doesn't enjoy making you sad or angry. He just knows that if you aren't disciplined you will continue going down a wrong path. You won't learn the right way. Discipline means you are loved.

Dear God, well, I don't like being disciplined. It isn't fun and it means that I've messed up. But, well, I'm glad You love me enough to discipline me. Amen.

Walking in the Light

God is light; in Him there is no darkness at all. If we claim to have fellowship with Him yet walk in the darkness, we lie and do not live by the truth.

1 John 1:5-6

Do you know the old saying, "You can't tell a book by the cover"? It means that the artwork on the cover may promise one thing, but inside the plot is totally different.

The same thing holds true of your walk with God. You can make all the claims you want about how much you pray and how often you read the Bible and how close you are to God … but you can't fool God. What's truly in your heart will be evident to God.

If evil things are living in your heart, then you can make all the claims you want about how much you are living for God. He will know the truth and the truth is that you have been lying.

Dear God, I don't want to live a lie. Help me to really walk in the light … Your light. Amen.

No Unbelievers Allowed

"Therefore I tell you, whatever you ask for in prayer, believe that you have received it, and it will be yours."

Mark 11:24

"... And dear God, please help ... y-a-w-n ... blah, blah, blah ..." Does that kinda sound like your prayers? When you pray, do you believe God hears you? Do you believe He cares? Do you believe He might actually answer your prayers? If you don't, then you're just praying because you think that's what you're supposed to do. Or, maybe you're hoping that God just might actually hear you and answer.

That's not the way the Bible says to pray. Jesus spoke these words in Mark 11 and He said that when you pray you should believe God hears you and that He will answer. That, my friend, is a command from the top!

Dear God, knowing You actually hear my prayers changes how I'm going to pray. I know now that prayer can make a difference. Amen.

Yahoo ... Gulp!

Pray continually; give thanks in all circumstances, for this is God's will for you in Christ Jesus.

1 Thessalonians 5:17-18

"Okay," you may say, "... I've heard this praying all the time stuff before. But, giving thanks in all circumstances ... really? Does it really mean *all* circumstances?"

Let's get real here. Is the Bible telling you to jump with joy when a loved one dies? What about if your friends start acting goofy and stop being friends with you? Well, yeah, that is what this verse says. But does God expect you to be *thankful* for rotten things that happen? No, but you *can* be thankful that you don't have to go through any of that stuff by yourself.

God knows everything that's going on. He will help you, strengthen you and never leave you alone. You can thank Him continually for that.

Dear God, thank You that You are always with me. Thank You for sticking close and giving me strength when things get rough. That helps. Amen.

Fish Food

From inside the fish Jonah prayed to the LORD his God.

Jonah 2:1

Have you ever messed up so bad that you thought things were hopeless? Well, you'd think that if anyone was going to be that low it would be Jonah. After all, he had disobeyed God, run away from Him, hidden in a boat and then ended up being swallowed by a fish.

But, as bad as things were, Jonah turned to God. He didn't wait to get to a nice, clean church to pray and ask God's forgiveness. Right there in the belly of the great fish, Jonah turned to God, confessed his sin and asked forgiveness. When you know you've messed up – the minute you know – get it straightened out with God. He will hear your prayer from wherever you are. He will forgive you and help you get back on track.

Dear God, sometimes it seems like I need a special place to pray. Help me to remember that I can pray anytime, anywhere and You will hear me. Amen.

Front Line Prayer

He answered their prayers,
because they trusted in Him.

1 Chronicles 5:20

Simple, huh? Trust God and He will answer your prayers. It might surprise you to know that this little nine-word sentence comes in the middle of the description of a terrible battle. Some soldiers cried out to God in the middle of a battle and He answered their prayers and helped them win.

The key here, though, is that these men trusted that God would hear their prayer and that He would answer. God rewarded their trust.

How much trust is involved in your prayers? It's easy to pray fancy prayers when things are going great. But, when you're in the middle of a battle, do you believe He hears your prayer? You should – His track record recorded in the Bible shows how much He cares.

Dear God, I don't know why it's so hard for me to trust You. Help me learn how to trust. Amen.

Pray for Peace

"Pray for those who mistreat you."

Luke 6:28

WHAT? Pray for the creeps who push me around, make fun of me and generally make life miserable? *No way*! Oh wait, maybe I will pray for them – pray that their hair falls out and they each get a zillion pimples – the kind that hurt! Umm, no, that won't work.

When Jesus said to pray for those who mistreat you, He meant to really pray for them. Prayer is conversation with God. Talking with God means your heart lines up with His and God's heart is filled with love.

You can't continue to be angry with someone you are praying for. So, praying for your enemies leads to peace in your own heart. Not a bad side benefit, eh?

Dear God, help me to be strong enough to pray for my enemies. I can't do it without Your help. Amen.

Never Alone

Teach me to do Your will, for You are my God;
may Your good Spirit lead me on level ground.

Psalm 143:10

"Hey, a little help here!" Ever feel like you're walking in complete darkness? So dark that you can't even see your hand in front of your face? You cry out for help but your words seem to bounce right back into your face. You feel alone. All alone.

Maybe you're crying out to the wrong people. Maybe you're looking for help in the wrong places. God will hear your prayers. He will teach you how to live and He will show you what His will is. He has promised that His Holy Spirit will lead you. You're not alone. God wants to help you. He's just waiting for you to ask. Go on … ask.

Dear God, I need Your help. Just like the psalmist, I am asking You to help me and teach me. Thank You for never leaving me alone. Amen.

No Worries

Do not be anxious about anything,
but in everything, by prayer and petition,
with thanksgiving, present your requests to God.

Philippians 4:6

Cold sweat breaks out on your forehead. Breath comes in short, shallow gasps. Your senses are heightened so much that you think you can hear a pin hit the floor. You are ready to run at a moment's notice. What's going on? Fear – simple, heart-pounding fear. What makes you afraid? What makes you worry? What do you do with those emotions?

God says you should bring them to Him. After all, when you think about it, He's the only One who can actually do something about the things that worry or scare You. Trust Him enough to bring those things to Him. Don't worry ... pray!

Dear God, I waste a lot of energy worrying or being scared when all I really need to do is bring my fears to You. Thank You for caring. Help me to remember to come to You first ... then I won't need to worry later. Amen.

Number One

"If My people, who are called by My name, will humble themselves and pray and seek My face and turn from their wicked ways, then I will hear from heaven and will forgive their sin and will heal their land."

2 Chronicles 7:14

Have you ever wanted something so much that you could almost taste it? So much that you couldn't think about anything else? That thing you wanted or the attention of someone you cared about colored everything else.

Well, you can almost hear the longing in God's voice in this verse. He wants His people to turn to Him. God wants your love. He wants you to put aside your pride ... your own agenda ... to humble yourself before Him. He wants to be most important. He wants to forgive your sin.

All He asks is humbleness and prayer.

Dear God, I know that sometimes I'm more important to me than You are. Help me to learn to get myself out of the way and seek Your will. Amen.

38 Best Prayers

"When you pray, do not be like the hypocrites, for they love to pray standing in the synagogue and on the street corners to be seen by men."

Matthew 6:5

Show-offs, don't you hate 'em? People who always have to be the center of attention. No matter what's going on, they get louder and goofier so that everyone looks at them. They think they are so cool.

Is it hard to believe that some people actually show off when they are praying? Yeah, they pray long and loud and use fancy words. It "sounds" like they are super-spiritual. But what's in their hearts is not so pure. They are putting on a show for people ... not for God.

When you pray, don't put on a show for others, remember that you don't have to say fancy words and pray long prayers. Just pray what's in your heart.

Dear God, I love You. I want to pray what's in my heart and be honest with You. Thanks for hearing my prayers. Amen.

Make a Difference

The prayer of a righteous person is powerful and effective.

James 5:16

"I can't do anything, I'm just a kid." Nothing I think or say or do makes any difference to anyone." Is that what you think? Well, hold on there Miss Negative! It just isn't so. This verse promises that your prayers can make a difference in your life and the lives of others.

If your heart really desires to serve God – if it's righteous – your prayers make a difference. Don't view the "righteous" part of this as a negative. It doesn't mean you don't ever sin or do something wrong.

It means that in the center of your heart you truly desire to serve and obey God. He knows you're going to mess up sometimes. He doesn't expect perfection – it's not possible anyway. Keep your heart focused on God and pray for all you're worth – it makes a difference.

Dear God, thank You that I can make a difference by praying. We're quite a team. Amen.

40

Good Things

Praise the LORD, for the LORD is good;
sing praise to His name, for that is pleasant.

Psalm 135:3

Hey, when someone starts saying nice things about you, do you tell them to stop or do you eat it up? It makes you feel good to hear nice things about yourself. It's nice to know you are appreciated and that people see your good qualities or your efforts to do nice things.

Good reminder – don't make all your prayers, "God, do this or help that or give me." Take time every day to thank God for what He does for you. Praise Him for His loving kindness, for giving you your family, friends, home. Praise Him for the world He created. Praise Him for taking care of you. Praise Him for having a plan for your life. Praise Him every day.

Dear God, I'm sorry that my prayers are so often "Give me ..." I do praise You for Your love and care. Amen.

Prayer Partners

Go, gather together all the Jews who are in Susa, and fast for me. Do not eat or drink for three days, night or day. I and my maids will fast as you do.

Esther 4:16

Go without food for three days ... yeah, right ... and do what? Well, usually fasting is associated with praying. So, when Queen Esther asked Mordecai to have the Jews fast for her, she probably assumed they were praying for her, too. It worked and God helped her protect the Jewish people from being killed.

Queen Esther was smart – she knew she needed prayer support. She had a job to do that was too big to do alone. Most jobs are.

Everyone needs the prayers of others to help them through life. Talk to someone you trust about being your prayer partner. Share things with each other and pray for each other.

Dear God, help me to find a good prayer partner ... someone who will pray with me about things. Amen.

Prayer and Praise

About midnight Paul and Silas were praying and singing hymns to God, and the other prisoners were listening to them.

Acts 16:25

How nice. Paul and Silas had a prison ministry – visiting the prisoners and having a praise and worship time for them. *Not quite!* Paul and Silas *were* prisoners. Their feet were in chains. They couldn't get up and walk around. They hadn't done anything wrong. They just preached about God and were thrown into prison.

Why on earth were they praying and singing when they were in prison? They knew that prayer and praise are not just for when things are going great. They had an audience of prisoners who needed to know that God loved them. Paul and Silas didn't waste time feeling sorry for themselves. How do you react when life gets tough? Remember that others are listening to you.

Dear God, I forgot that others are listening. Help me to act like Paul and Silas. Amen.

Give 'em Up

Cast all your anxiety on Him
because He cares for you.

1 Peter 5:7

What kinds of things do you worry about? What keeps you awake at night with a knot in your stomach the size of Toledo?

Stop and think about it – does any of the stuff you worry about actually happen? Most of it doesn't, so why spend so much time worrying? It's easy to simply say ... *stop worrying*. But it's hard to let it go 'cause you have to have somewhere to put that energy.

The best thing to do is to put that energy into prayer. Give your problems and worries to God. He cares about what worries you and He can take care of it. Just give it to Him.

Dear God, it's hard to let go of the things that worry or scare me. Help me to be able to give those things to You and just leave them there. Amen.

Just Ask

"Ask and it will be given to you; seek and you will find; knock and the door will be opened to you. For everyone who asks receives; he who seeks finds; and to him who knocks, the door will be opened."

Matthew 7:7-8

When someone makes a promise to you, do you absolutely believe that they will keep that promise? Do you plan on it and start living as if it's already done? Some people aren't so good at keeping promises or maybe they keep a promise halfway. But you can plan on God's promises.

These words in Matthew were spoken by Jesus. Sounds like there's a whole lot of stuff that people don't have just because they don't ask for it. God wants to give you so much because He loves you. Line your heart up with Him and ask for His blessings and guidance in life.

Dear God, I don't want to miss stuff just because I didn't ask. Please help me to keep asking You for guidance and help. Amen.

Wait, Wait, Wait!

I waited patiently for the LORD;
He turned to me and heard my cry.

Psalm 40:1

Waiting is not fun! Are you a patient waiter who goes quietly about life until the things happen you've been waiting for? How about with God? Do you ask God to do something or help with something, then get tired of waiting and take matters into your own hands?

Here's a news flash – you can't take care of things as well as He can. The psalmist learned that it was important to wait patiently for God. David cried out to God – poured out the feelings in his heart – then waited and God heard his prayers. Waiting is not fun. It's not easy. But, when you wait, you have time to learn to trust God and to think about if you really want Him to do what you asked in the heat of the moment.

Dear God, I'm too impatient. Help me to be more patient. Help me to learn to trust You more. Amen.

Needs vs. Wants

My God will meet all your needs according to His glorious riches in Christ Jesus.

Philippians 4:19

Does this sound familiar ... "I need new shoes," or "I need an MP3 player" or "I need a cell-phone?" Now, stop and think about how many times you tell your parents you *need* something. Do you really need those things or do you simply *want* them? Are your prayers want-based instead of need-based? Often we try to tell God what to do because we want our lives to be easier or happier. We ask Him to do things the way we *want*.

God hasn't promised to do that. He promised to supply our needs. That's a whole different thing. Think about it – has God supplied your needs? Most likely. Stop and thank Him for knowing what's best for you and supplying those things.

Dear God, this is hard. Thank You for supplying my needs and for understanding when I pray for what I want. Amen.

Forgive and Forget

"When you stand praying, if you hold anything against anyone, forgive him, so that your Father in heaven may forgive you your sins."

Mark 11:25

Hey ... who do you think you are? Do you really think it's okay to talk to God – telling Him how sorry you are for the wrong things you've done and asking Him to forgive you when you're holding anger in your heart toward someone? Get real. If you dare to ask God to forgive your sins, you'd better be willing to forgive others for whatever they have done.

There's an old saying that says what's good for the goose is good for the gander – yeah, strange, but what it means is that if God is kind and forgiving enough to forgive you, then you should certainly forgive others. Come to God with a pure heart so He can forgive you and bless you.

Dear God, I guess that makes sense. Help me be forgiving of others. Actually, I'll be glad to get rid of the anger anyway. It takes a lot of energy to hold a grudge. Amen.

Strength and Courage

When I called, You answered me;
You made me bold and stouthearted.

Psalm 138:3

Ever feel like you're on your own? Like no one understands you? And no one can really do anything about the junk in your life anyway. Maybe you turn to your friends for help ... and they can't do anything. The bottom line is even the people who love you can't fix the problems in your life. That job is God's and God's alone. Call on Him. Ask Him to give you courage and wisdom. Ask Him to walk with you through life. He will. He promised.

The psalmist found that out. God answered his cry and made him strong and courageous. You can handle a lot in life when you know you aren't alone!

Dear God, thank You for hearing my prayers. Help me to remember that You do and help me find strength and courage in knowing that I'm not alone. Amen.

Adoration

Give thanks to the LORD, for He is good.
His love endures forever.

Psalm 136:1

Who is your favorite singing group? Have you ever gone to one of their concerts? Did the crowd shout and scream? Do you have posters of the singer up in your room? Do you try to dress like them, wear your hair like them? Do you admire everything they say and do? Know what? Only God is worthy of being adored like that.

That's a part of prayer that just can't be ignored – adoring God for who He is and for all He does for you. Stop and think about the stories in the Bible of God's care for His people. Think about the miracles He did to protect them over and over. Look around at the beautiful world He made. Remember that He thought of families, friends, pets ... all the things that fill your life with joy. Adore Him for His creativity and generosity.

Dear God, I do adore You. Thank You for all You have done for me and given me. Amen.

Confession Is Good

If we confess our sins, He is faithful
and just and will forgive us our sins
and purify us from all unrighteousness.

1 John 1:9

When you get the order to clean your room from your mom, do you ever just stuff a bunch of junk under the bed or in your closet so the floor looks clean? Do you ever throw clean clothes into the laundry hamper instead of hanging them up?

Yeah, covering up stuff is not the same as cleaning. The same is true with prayer. God says you should confess your sin – admit what you've done wrong. Don't try to cover it up, just confess. When you do, He promises to forgive you and cleanse you.

That's a good trade-off for honesty, right?

Dear God, it's hard to admit that I've done wrong things. I guess I think that if I don't admit it, maybe You won't notice. That is the wrong way to think. Okay, I'm sorry for my sin. Please forgive me. Amen.

Teamwork!

Be alert and always keep
on praying for all the saints.

Ephesians 6:18

A basketball or soccer team only wins games if all the players work together. If there's a superstar who doesn't help his teammates or pass the ball to them, then the team won't win many games. Teammates need each other. God's children need each other, too. That's why the Bible tells us to pray for each other. Your prayers for other Christians will help them be strong and stay close to God.

Your prayers will help you feel close to others, too – you'll feel like a teammate as you hold your friends and family members up in prayer before God. You'll also feel like you have a part in their walk with God. Pray for others – all the time!

Dear God, I need others' prayers and I want to remember to pray for others. Thanks for the team! Amen.

Prayer Helper

He who searches our hearts knows the mind of the Spirit, because the Spirit intercedes for the saints in accordance with God's will.

Romans 8:27

No doubt you believe prayer is important. After all, you've probably heard about prayer ever since you started going to church or Sunday school. But, have you ever been in a place where the problems in your life are so overwhelming that you just don't know what to pray – you can't find the words to make sense of what you're feeling?

Not to worry. Remember that Jesus asked God to send the Holy Spirit to always be with believers. Well, the Holy Spirit doesn't just hang out with you – He prays for you! When You can't find the words to say what's in your heart, the Holy Spirit will pray for you! He knows exactly what you need.

Dear God, thank You so much for the Holy Spirit. Thank You for His prayers for me. I'm thankful for His help. Amen.

World Leaders

I urge, then, first of all, that requests, prayers, intercession and thanksgiving be made for everyone – for kings and all those in authority, that we may live peaceful and quiet lives in all godliness and holiness.

1 Timothy 2:1-2

Did you know that you can play a part in world decisions? Yeah, presidents, senators, representatives, kings, prime ministers ... people who make decisions that affect the whole world need your prayers. Do you think to pray for them?

These verses encourage you to pray for those in authority. After all, they need God a lot! They make decisions about wars, taxes and normal everyday life for everyone. When you pray for God to lead and guide them, that puts you on their team and that gives you a part in their work. Remember to pray for these world leaders to follow God and to lead their nations with the wisdom He gives.

Dear God. I pray that the leaders of my country will follow You closely. Amen.

Best News Ever

Pray for us that the message of the Lord may spread rapidly and be honored, just as it was with you.

2 Thessalonians 3:1

When you hear some really good news, what's the first thing you do? Probably hop on the phone and call a friend to tell her the good news, right? What kinds of things do you and your friends talk about? News about other people; about singing groups; about school? News about those kinds of things spreads pretty quickly.

But the most important news in the world; the most important news in all of history should be the quickest spreading news – the news of God's love. Remember to pray for people who have made it their life's work to share that good news. Pray for the message to spread around the world. It's the most important message ever!

Dear God, help missionaries around the world do their work to tell people about You. Help my minister, too, as he works right here in our town. Amen.

Praise God!

Praise the LORD. Praise God in His sanctuary ...
praise Him for His acts of power ...
praise Him with the sounding of the trumpet ...
let everything that has breath praise the LORD.

Psalm 150

Yahoo for God! Praise God all the time. Praise God everywhere. Praise Him with every breath. Forget about asking God for stuff. Forget about complaining. Just stop and praise Him.

Let your mind and heart fill up with thoughts of how loving and kind He is. Think about His power. Think about His creativity and His gifts to you. Dance around and sing a joyful song of praise to Him. Go ahead – you'll enjoy it – and so will God!

Dear God, I praise You for mountains and oceans. I praise You for flowers, butterflies, puppies and kittens. I praise You for my family and my friends. I praise You for loving me and taking care of me. I praise You for everything! Amen.

Daily Bread

"Give us each day our daily bread."

Luke 11:3

Some people never have enough of anything. They want more money, a bigger house, a nicer car ... what about you? Are you always wanting more clothes, more CDs ... more stuff? When do you have enough?

Jesus taught an example of how to pray. It's known as the Lord's Prayer. He taught us to pray for our daily bread – what we *need* for each day. That's all. His prayer example reminds us that some people don't have enough food to eat for one day, but others store food up so they have supplies for months and months. Some people pray for just a piece of bread for today while others have fancy houses, cars and so much stuff that ... well, it's embarrassing.

Pray for what you *need*, not for excess. And, thank God for what He gives you.

Dear God, thank You for giving me food for each day. Thank You for all You give me. Amen.

Cleaned Up

"Forgive us our sins, for we also
forgive everyone who sins against us."

Luke 11:4

Say it's a hot summer's day and you've been out playing soccer. You're dirty, sweaty and your hair is messy. Then, it's time to go to a friend's birthday party. Do you just go in your dirty, sweaty condition? Of course not; you take a shower, wash your hair and put on clean clothes. You get cleaned up.

Getting cleaned up is part of a healthy prayer life, too. When you pray, don't immediately hit God with a lot of "gimmes and do this stuff," get cleaned up first. Confess your sins and ask His forgiveness. Clean up your whole heart by forgiving people you've been holding a grudge against. Once you're cleaned up, you can praise Him and bring your requests to Him.

Dear God, help me to remember to get cleaned up at the beginning of my talks with You. Amen.

Mountain Movers

"If you have faith and do not doubt ... you can say to this mountain, 'Go, throw yourself into the sea,' and it will be done."

Matthew 21:21

Do you believe you can lift a 500 lb weight ... with one hand? Yeah, you probably *don't* believe that your one arm has that much strength. Well, how about your prayers. Do you believe that your prayers have any power at all? Maybe you don't bother to pray for things that seem impossible because you just don't believe God can do what you want or that He will do what you want.

What's amazing is that there is so much power available to us if we just believe! Think about it – you could move a mountain if you really had faith and didn't doubt. Try it!

Dear God, I want to make a difference in the world. Help my faith to grow. Help me to believe that You hear my prayers and that You will answer! Amen.

Focus, Focus, Focus

Teach me Your way, O LORD,
and I will walk in Your truth; give me
an undivided heart, that I may fear Your name.

Psalm 86:11

Do you know someone who is "best friends" with you when you're together, but when you're not, she talks about you to others? That stinks, doesn't it?

Well, imagine how God feels when His children have a divided heart. One minute they're praising Him and asking His help with stuff, but the next minute they're trashing somebody or using God's name as a swear word, or being unkind or stealing ... anything that is the opposite of walking in the truth.

Don't be guilty of a divided heart. Ask God to teach you to walk in His ways and to keep your heart on track.

Dear God, sometimes my heart is divided. Sometimes I live for You and sometimes I don't. Teach me how to always live for You and to keep my heart focused on You. Amen.

First Call

Is any one of you in trouble? He should pray.
Is anyone happy? Let him sing songs of praise.

James 5:13

Honesty time – where do you go when you're in trouble? Do you call a friend or text message her? Do you spill your guts and cry and try to figure out an answer with her? You're going to the wrong place. God is where your help is. When you've got troubles, take them to Him. He cares and He can see the big picture of how this problem might make you stronger. He won't let your troubles kill you. But He will let you learn from them.

Also, when you're happy and things are going great, remember to praise Him. The bottom line is – talk to God every day, about everything!

Dear God, sometimes talking to You isn't my first thought. It might even be my fourth or fifth thought. I'm sorry. I know You love me and care about what's happening. I'll come to You first – when I need help and when I'm happy! Amen.

Not An Option

"Go and make disciples of all nations, baptizing them in the name of the Father and of the Son and of the Holy Spirit and teaching them to obey everything I have commanded you."

Matthew 28:19-20

Sharing the message of God's love is not an option. You can't shrug your shoulders and say, "That's for grown-ups to do." It doesn't say, "Everyone over twenty-five should go and make disciples ..." Nope, the truth is that kids might listen to someone their own age better than they would an adult. This doesn't mean you have to stand behind a pulpit and preach a sermon. You can start being a witness by just living your life for God.

There's an old saying that your life may be the only Bible some people will ever read. Don't be afraid to make choices that reflect your love for God and obedience to Him.

Dear God, help me live so that others can see my love for You. Amen.

Ripples

"You will receive power when the Holy Spirit comes on you; and you will be My witnesses in Jerusalem, and in all Judea and Samaria, and to the ends of the earth."

Acts 1:8

Witnessing is like ripples. You know, when you toss a pebble into a puddle of water, the ripples start small around where the pebble went into the water. Then they get larger as they spread out from that spot. Jesus said you should start witnessing right where you are – with your close friends and family. That's your Jerusalem.

Then the ripples spread to your Judea – your school, and your larger group of friends. Then you may get a chance to go to Samaria and the ends of the earth on short-term mission trips or things like that. You never know what God has planned for you. For right now ... just take care of your Jerusalem.

Dear God, witnessing kind of scares me. Help me live in a way that shows how much I love You. Give me the right words when I get a chance to share. Thanks. Amen.

Stop, Look and Worship

Then those who were in the boat worshiped Him, saying, "Truly You are the Son of God."

Matthew 14:33

What is a witness? Simply stated, a witness is someone who has seen something. The disciples saw Jesus do all kinds of miracles. This verse describes their response to seeing Him walking on the water to their boat. They worshiped Him. "Well, duh," you say, "if God did some super-miracle for me, I'd worship Him, too." Well, duh, yourself.

Look around you. God does miracles for you every day – the sun comes up, the stars stay in their places, the oceans don't overrun the earth, you have a family who loves you, He helps you make choices that keep you in one piece. You've gotten so used to miracles that you expect them to happen day after day. Stop, look and worship Him for them.

Dear God, I guess I do have stuff to witness about. Stuff that You do for me every day. Help me remember that and share it with others and … thanks. Amen.

Fear Not!

"Be strong and very courageous. Be careful to obey all the law My servant Moses gave you; do not turn from it to the right or to the left, that you may be successful wherever you go."

Joshua 1:7

Oral book reviews ... words that strike fear in the hearts of students! Public speaking is one of the biggest fears people have. Guess it makes sense that witnessing would be included in that. There is the fear of sharing your faith in public, fear of them rejecting what you say – or worse – making fun of you, and the fear of not getting it right. Whew! Lots to be afraid of.

Take courage and start with what you know. Obey the Ten Commandments and that obedience and love for others will set you apart from the world. Your life will become a witness before you ever have to speak a word.

Dear God, help me remember that my friends will notice how I live and what I say. Help me to be a witness for You. Amen.

Excitement!

The disciples were overjoyed
when they saw the Lord.

John 20:20

Christmas morning. Presents are piled around the tree – big ones and small ones. One package could be ... might be ... the one thing you want so much you can taste it.

The family slowly makes its way through the gift-opening and finally, that one box is in front of you – wonder of wonders! It is exactly what you wanted. *You are overjoyed!* You can't wait to tell your friends ... every one of them!

When you know something that is great news or when you get something that is awesome, you want to tell people! That's where witnessing comes in. When the disciples understood who Jesus was, they wanted to tell people. What's your response when you get excited about God's love for you?

Dear God, I want to be excited about You. I want to be so excited that I just tell everyone! Amen.

Harvest Time!

"The harvest is plentiful but the workers are few. Ask the Lord of the harvest, therefore, to send out workers into His harvest field."

Matthew 9:37-38

What would happen if a farmer had fields of grain ready to be harvested, but no workers to pick the grain? Everything in the fields would all rot and go to waste. God's harvest is the people of the world – the people who need to know Him in order to be saved. There are literally hundreds of thousands of people who might choose to accept Jesus, but ... no one has told them about Him. The workers are few – some people aren't doing their job of being Christ's witnesses. It's not a job for just certain people; it's a job for everyone who believes in Jesus. How are you doing at this job?

Dear God, it's kinda scary to tell people about You. Please help me. Give me the right words to say and the courage to say them. Amen.

Do Your Job

I planted the seed, Apollos watered it, but God made it grow.

1 Corinthians 3:6

"Witness? You want me to tell someone about God? You want me to help someone be saved? I can't do that. I'm just a kid. Are you crazy? It's too much!" Alright ... calm down, kid. You don't have to do it all by yourself. Witnessing and helping people get saved is a team effort.

Maybe you plant the seed by just living your life for Christ. Maybe someone else waters it by sharing Bible verses with the same person. But, only God can bring a person to Himself.

Sometimes you might be the seed planter. Sometimes you might be the water girl. The point is ... you are willing to do what God wants you to do.

Dear God, when I see that witnessing is a team thing, that makes it easier. Help me to just take the opportunities You give me. Amen.

Best Kept Secret

Praise the LORD. Give thanks to the LORD, for He is good; His love endures forever.

Psalm 106:1

Praising God cannot be a private thing. If you just worship and praise Him in the privacy of your room or even in the safety of your church, well you are missing something. The truth is that if you're embarrassed or scared of what your friends might think about your relationship with God, then you probably don't feel free to really worship Him.

If you can't praise Him and thank Him with all your heart, then it's going to be pretty hard to tell others about Him. So, where are you on this? Is God the best kept secret you ever had?

Dear God. Okay, I admit that sometimes I'm nervous about what my friends think about me being a Christian. Help me to get over it and let my love for You grow. Amen.

Time Is Running Out

"As long as it is day, we must do the work of Him who sent Me. Night is coming, when no one can work."

John 9:4

When you have a big project to do for school, do you wait until the last minute to start it? Then you stay up all night writing the papers and gathering your visuals, checking your references and hoping that you get it finished. If you've waited too late to start, well, you run out of time.

That's the point Jesus was making in this verse. Some people look around at their family and friends and think, "Yeah, they need to hear about God, but there will be time to tell them later." Jesus' reminder is that eventually time runs out and it will be too late to witness. Do the work while it's still day time!

Dear God, I guess I've thought that there will always be another chance to tell my friends about You. I know now that time is going to run out eventually. Help me to get busy! Amen.

Salty!

"You are the salt of the earth. But if the salt loses its saltiness, how can it be made salty again? It is no longer good for anything, except to be thrown out and trampled by men."

Matthew 5:13

You're different ... well, you're supposed to be. As much as you try to dress like everyone else, have the same brand of shoes, same kind of backpack, like the same music ... all those things ... you're supposed to be different. What does salt do for food? Gives it flavor. It prevents it from spoiling.

Jesus said that you ... one of His children ... can do those same things. You should be different in the way you treat others, even your parents, how you respect authority, how you handle problems. You should give a God-like flavor to your world. That's witnessing with your life.

Dear God, to be salt I need to be thinking about You all the time – even when it's hard and I'm hanging out with my friends. Help me to be salt to them. Amen.

Light Up the World!

"You are the light of the world.
A city on a hill cannot be hidden."

Matthew 5:14

A light shining in darkness can be seen from a great distance – even a small light! It lights up everything around it – things can be seen that would be lost in the darkness. Jesus said that a Christian (that's you, kiddo) is a light in a world full of people who are literally dying.

People will eventually come toward the light because the darkness gets pretty discouraging. Witnessing doesn't have to be a big scary thing. It's just living – living in obedience to God. It means you can't act one way with your friends and another way at church. It's important that you live for God all the time. Be a light.

Dear God, it's so hard to live for You in front of my friends sometimes. Help me, please. Give me courage. Amen.

Living Real

"For I tell you that unless your righteousness surpasses that of the Pharisees and the teachers of the law, you will certainly not enter the kingdom of heaven."

Matthew 5:20

Fakin' it – ever tried it? You know, pretending that you like someone when you really don't. Faking that you've studied for a test when you haven't. Or faking that you pray every day and really care about what God wants for you.

You can fool people. You can even fake witnessing about who God is. But, you can't fool God. He looks at the heart and knows what your motives are.

The Pharisees were fakers. They acted religious, but in their hearts they didn't care at all about God. If you're just faking your relationship with God, don't bother. No, just stop it and get real. Live for God and let your life be a witness for Him.

Dear God, I don't want to be a faker. Help me be real. Amen.

In Training

For the eyes of the LORD range throughout the earth
to strengthen those whose hearts
are fully committed to Him.

2 Chronicles 16:9

Getting prepared. That's key. A weight-lifter doesn't start his career by lifting 500 pounds. A marathoner doesn't run 26 miles the first time she puts on her running shoes. An athlete of any kind begins her career by training. She builds up her muscles and her lung strength in preparation to be able to do her best.

Aren't you glad to hear that the same thing is true in the Christian life? You are in training! You start by giving your heart to God and He keeps strengthening you to do His work. He's always watching out for you, too. He's watching to see when you need His help.

Dear God, thank You for strengthening me. Thank You for helping me. Amen.

Live with Purpose

So then, each of us will give
an account of himself to God.

Romans 14:12

What does it mean to give an account? Well, every month the bank sends a report of what is in your bank account. That is an account. Giving an account of your life to God means that you explain what you have been doing with your life. How are you spending your time and energy? God's going to ask you.

You see, God has given people a basic job to do – obey Him and live for Him and share the news with people around you. The day will come when God will ask you to give an account of your life. Begin right now to live your life with purpose so your accounting will be good.

Dear God, I want to live on purpose so my accounting to You will be good. Please help me. Amen.

Witness to Love

They will tell of the glory of Your kingdom and speak of Your might, so that all men may know of Your mighty acts and the glorious splendor of Your kingdom.

Psalm 145:11-12

So … do you think, "I can't witness about God. I wouldn't know what to talk about." These two verses are a clue. When you witness you talk about the glory of His kingdom and His might. Don't you think your friends and family would be happy to learn about God's kingdom – a perfect place filled with love. It's also a comfort to think about His mighty acts because they show His power.

Maybe you don't feel like you see His power in your own everyday life, but you do see it in nature and you know the stories in the Bible. You can witness about those. Most of all, you should witness about His constant, wonderful love.

Dear God, I know You love me. Help me to tell others that You love them, too. Amen.

Never Too Young

The LORD said to me, "Do not say 'I am only a child.' You must go to everyone I send you to and say whatever I command you ... I have put My words in your mouth."

Jeremiah 1:7, 9

Jeremiah was one of the greatest prophets who ever served God. But, when God first called him to serve, Jeremiah said, "I can't serve You, I'm too young!" He wasn't, of course, because anyone of any age can serve God.

God has called you, too, to do something for Him. It may not be to preach or teach ... it might be to just be friends with someone who needs to know that God loves her.

Whatever He wants you to do, if you stay close to Him by reading His Word and praying, He will give you the words to speak when the time is right.

Dear God, wow, even Jeremiah thought he was too young. I guess if You helped him, You will help me, too. Amen.

Growing Up!

The way of a fool seems right to him,
but a wise man listens to advice.

Proverbs 12:15

The *terrible twos!* Parents hear stories about how stubborn their darling little children are going to become when they hit two years old ... and it's usually true. But then as the child gets a little older she gets a bit wiser and begins to want to learn and she listens to advice.

Sometimes it's scary to think about telling your friends about the Lord because you think they wouldn't care anyway. Be careful about that. Sometimes they want to learn. They want advice on how to live in this world. They just might be waiting to hear what you have to say!

Dear God, I never thought of that. Maybe my friends are just waiting for me to tell them about You. Give me the right time and the right words to tell them! Amen.

The Most Important Topic

The Lord is my helper; I will not be afraid.

Hebrews 13:6

You can probably talk with your friends about anything – problems with your parents – how they totally do not understand you – that their rules are old-fashioned; that you have way too many chores to do; teachers – good ones and bad ones – too much homework; people at school – cool ones and totally weird ones; clothes, music ... well, on and on.

But the one topic that is hardest to bring up is definitely the most important – God. It's scary because you don't want your friends to feel like you think you're better than them. You don't want them to think you're the weird one! What do you do about this fear? Pray ... ask God to help you. Then, remember that He will help and there is nothing to be afraid of!

Dear God, okay. Help me talk with my friends about You. Give me the courage to speak up. Amen.

The Real You

Jesus said to them, "Only in his hometown and in his own house is a prophet without honor."

Matthew 13:57

One place where it's very hard to talk about Jesus is ... at home. After all, your parents and brothers and sisters know the *real you*. They know your temper fits, when you tell a little lie or don't do your chores. They see your bad attitudes and the times you aren't loving. It's hard to talk about God and live for Him when these people see the times you don't.

That's okay, Jesus knew it would be hard. He knew that the people you love the most would be the hardest to talk to about Him. Ask Him to help you live in a loving and obedient way so your family will notice.

Dear God, sometimes my family makes me so mad. But I do really love them and I want them to know You. Help me live for You in front of them – all the time. Amen.

God Knows

"Do you understand what you are reading?"
Philip asked. "How can I," he said,
"unless someone explains it to me?"

Acts 8:30-31

Philip was just walking along the road, minding his own business, when God told him to talk to this guy. Philip was confused because the guy was a government official – kinda scary to talk about God to someone so important. But, what do ya know? The guy was actually reading the Bible but he didn't understand it. So, Philip explained it to him and the guy got it!

When you feel that nudge to talk to someone about God – don't fight it. God knows the whole picture of what that person is going through and what they are thinking about. He knows when the time is right. Don't question Him, just obey!

Dear God, help me listen and obey. Help me remember that You know the whole story. Amen.

Proving Your Work

Always be prepared to give an answer to everyone who asks you to give the reason for the hope that you have.

1 Peter 3:15

Are you able to come up with the right answer to a complicated math problem? Then the teacher asks you to prove your work, show how you arrived at the answer. Sometimes that's the hard part.

Maybe you're pretty good at living the Christian life. For the most part you are able to control gossiping and bad attitudes. Maybe you're pretty good at letting your friends see that you trust God. But, at some point one of them may ask you why your life is different. Gulp. You need to have answers ready to give them. Pray about that right now and ask the Lord to help you be ready to give that answer.

Dear God, I thought that if I just live right that's enough and I'll never have to actually say anything ... so, would You help me be ready with the right words? Thanks. Amen.

Ambassadors

We are therefore Christ's ambassadors,
as though God were making His appeal through us.

2 Corinthians 5:20

What does an ambassador do? An ambassador from one country goes to another country to spread good feelings about his homeland. He is a representative. You have the opportunity to be Christ's ambassador – spread good feelings and good news about Him.

Actually, whether you admit it or not you are an ambassador for something. Either you stand for Christ or you stand against Him. There really isn't a middle of the road here.

Not making a choice to serve Him is to actually make a choice NOT to serve Him. Take on the responsibility and recognize that you are His ambassador – live strong for Him!

Dear God, I want to be the best ambassador You've ever had. Help me live strong for You! Amen.

Instant Witness

Leaving her water jar, the woman went back to the town and said to the people, "Come, see a man who told me everything I ever did. Could this be the Christ?"

John 4:28-29

Stubborn love. That's what Jesus had for this woman. She had a messy life. She had been married several times and was living with some dude she wasn't married to. She had made bad choices. Plus, she had a rotten attitude. Here she was talking to Jesus Himself ... and she was pretty snippy! Jesus didn't walk away though.

He kept talking, kept loving and finally the walls around her heart broke open. Then, what did she do? Ran to tell others about Him! She became an instant witness. That's what excitement does. That's what joy does. That's what understanding does. Do you understand how much He loves you? Do you understand how much He loves everyone? Then ... tell them!

Dear God, I want to be as excited as this woman was. Fill me with joy and excitement. Amen.

One Way!

Salvation is found in no one else,
for there is no other name under heaven
given to men by which we must be saved.

Acts 4:12

A one-way sign beside the road means ... you can only go in one direction on that street. If you try to go the other way, you'll get a ticket and probably cause an accident. There are lots of "ways to get to heaven" being thrown around in our world today. Maybe some of your friends have embraced some of those ideas. The sad thing is that they aren't true. The way to heaven is through accepting Jesus as Savior.

One way – no other doors and no other paths. You've got the truth! Cool, huh? But you also must find a way to share that truth with your friends. Don't let them believe a lie.

Dear God, give me the words to speak and the right time to speak them. I want my friends to know You. Amen.

Anyone Can Be Saved

All those who heard him were astonished and asked, "Isn't he the man who raised havoc in Jerusalem among those who call on this [Christ's] name?

Acts 9:21

Saul was a nasty guy. He made it his life's work to find people who believed in Christ and make their lives *miserable*. He was good at it, too. If there ever was a person you would think could not be saved, it would be Saul. But, lo and behold, Jesus got hold of Saul's heart and it was changed. Saul became Paul – one of the greatest preachers of all time and the guy God used to write lots of the Bible.

Do you know someone who is so bad that you think she could never be saved? Someone so mean that you think she would never want to know about God? Don't be so sure. Changing the heart is God's work, not yours.

Dear God, I'll leave the heart changing to You. I'll just do what You want me to do and not worry if the people I talk to decide to follow You. Amen.

The Beginning

All have sinned and fall short of the glory of God.

Romans 3:23

Basic information here. Everyone who ever lived on this earth is a sinner. That began with Adam and Eve. Everyone needs to know that Jesus came to earth, lived and taught, was crucified, died and rose again. He did all this for one reason – love.

The fact is that the good things people do won't get them into heaven. The good things they do don't mean they aren't sinners anymore. Everyone probably knows deep in their own hearts that they have bad thoughts and selfish motives. What people need to realize is that God knows that, too.

This is basic information that a person must understand before she believes she needs God in her life.

Dear God, I can always explain away my sin and I guess others do, too. Help me understand this basic information in my life and be able to explain it to others. We are sinners … all of us. Amen.

The Price Is Paid

The wages of sin is death, but the gift of God is eternal life in Christ Jesus our Lord.

Romans 6:23

"You get what you pay for." You may buy a shirt that looks exactly like a designer brand. It isn't though, it's a knock-off brand that is a lot cheaper. But, after a while you may discover that it doesn't hold up as well as the real thing. The seams come loose or it loses its shape or the color fades – well, you got what you paid for.

The same is true of sin. If a person chooses to live a sinful life, ignoring God, there is a price to pay – eternal death. No heaven.

The good news you can share with others is that God took care of that. He paid the price for you! Jesus' death and resurrection opened the door to heaven and eternal life! Good news to tell everyone, right?

Dear God, thank You for opening that door. It's good news that I want to tell others. Amen.

No Grudges

God demonstrates His own love for us in this: While we were still sinners, Christ died for us.

Romans 5:8

If you have a sister or brother, you know that sometimes life gets nasty at home. Your little brother can be a real creep and make you so stinking mad that you just want to lock him in the bathroom for about five years! So, when you're really angry at someone who has been mean to you, are you ever tempted to do something nice for him … for no reason? Yeah, probably not.

But think about this. People are sinners … all people. Even knowing that people were going to continually disobey Him and disappoint Him, God showed His incredible love by sending His Son, Jesus, to die for our sins. That's news worth sharing.

Dear God, wow, that's amazing. I need to tell others how much You love them. Amen.

Serious Stuff

If anyone's name was not found written in the book of life, he was thrown into the lake of fire.

Revelation 20:15

God does not deal in empty threats. Some people make empty threats like "Clean your room or you're grounded ... get your grades up or you'll be yanked out of school." Empty threats – some could be carried out and some couldn't. But, pretty soon you don't believe any of the threats that person gives.

Well, hear this – when God says that a person has to accept Jesus to come to heaven, that's no empty threat. Hell is a real place and if God's children don't witness to people so they know about God's love, well, their names will not be in the book of life ... and they won't be able to come into heaven. Serious stuff.

Dear God, sometimes it's hard to believe that hell is a real place. I don't want any of the people I love to go there. Help me tell them about You. Amen.

Domino Effect

You have made known to me the path of life;
You will fill me with joy in Your presence,
with eternal pleasures at Your right hand.

Psalm 16:11

Have you ever set dominos or blocks up in a long row? When you tip the first one it falls and knocks down all the ones behind it. That's the domino effect.

God never intended for it to be hard for people to know how to get to heaven. He gave us a whole book of instructions. He told His children to spread the news. God would be thrilled if every single person who ever lived had their name in the book of life. Each person has to choose to follow God, but they can't choose until they know about Him. That's where God's children come in – witnessing – telling others about God's love. Somebody told you the Good News, shouldn't you tell someone else? Pass on the Good News!

Dear God, I understand my responsibility. Help me know what to say and when to say it. Amen.

Get Off the Fence

Blessed is the man who fears the LORD,
who finds great delight in His commands.

Psalm 112:1

There is an old saying that goes, "Stand for something or you'll fall for anything." Step number one in becoming the best you that you can be is to decide what foundation you're going to stand on. Will you choose to obey God and honor Him even if family and friends around you do not?

If you've been riding the fence – acting one way when you hang out with certain friends and another way when you're with your church friends – well, that won't cut it.

Make a choice to obey God. That's the foundation to build the rest of your life on!

Dear Lord, okay, so I have to make a choice. Trying to keep a foot in both worlds is a lot of work anyway. I choose You. Amen.

Watch Your Mouth

He who guards his lips guards his life,
but he who speaks rashly will come to ruin.

Proverbs 13:3

Words can get you into so much trouble! From losing your temper and spouting off to gossip to just plain old unkind words. How many times have your feelings been hurt by what someone else has said? You know how hard it is to forget those unkind words. They lie on your heart like a steel blanket.

Your unkind words do the same thing to others. You don't want to be the reason someone is sad, discouraged or depressed, do you? Watch what you say. It's possible to speak in love, even when you are disagreeing with someone. You don't have to attack another person to disagree with her. Remember that you are God's representative, so, watch your mouth.

Dear Lord, sometimes words just seem to roll out of my mouth. Things I never meant to say. Help me to guard my mouth so I don't hurt other people. Amen.

Make a Change

Do not conform any longer to the pattern of this world, but be transformed by the renewing of your mind.

Romans 12:2

If you keep doing things the same old way, you're going to get the same old results. If you watch TV all day while eating chips and candy – you'll never lose weight and get physically fit. If you don't do your homework – you'll keep failing classes. You get the idea.

Becoming the best you possible may involve getting away from the habits and activities of your "old" life. Renew your mind by reading God's Word and talking with Him. Stop doing the things that you know are disobedient to Him.

You gotta make a choice to make a change.

Dear Lord, I want to change because I want to make a difference for You. Amen.

Sour Milk

"The good man brings good things out of the good stored up in his heart, and the evil man brings evil things out of the evil stored up in his heart. For out of the overflow of his heart his mouth speaks."

Luke 6:45

You are so hungry and thirsty that you think you just might faint. You grab some cookies and pour a glass of cold milk. You gobble up a cookie and take a big gulp of milk and ... *yuck*! The milk is sour. That stinks – it didn't look any different from fresh milk.

Yeah, things can look good on the outside, but when their insides are examined the truth comes out. If your heart is full of bad stuff like selfishness and anger, it's going to show on the outside, usually through the words you speak.

Take care of your heart.

Dear Lord, I know that some of the stuff in my heart is bad. Help me get rid of that stuff and fill my heart with love. Amen.

What Really Matters

If I give all I possess to the poor and surrender my body to the flames, but have not love, I gain nothing.

1 Corinthians 13:3

After a big disaster people around the world become very generous. They volunteer their services. Others send money. Still others send food and clothing. Maybe you've done some of these things, too. Good for you, we should help our neighbors around the world.

But, here's a question. How do you treat your family members? How do you feel about the grumpy old man that lives next door? It's a little easier to love people half way around the world than it is to love the ones you see every day.

Over and over in the Bible we are told to love one another ... love one another ... love. The people you see every day are the ones who need your love the most.

Dear Lord, some of the people around me are so hard to love. I'm gonna need Your help with this. Amen.

Calm Faith

The LORD will keep you from all harm – He will watch over your life; the LORD will watch over your coming and going both now and forevermore.

Psalm 121:7-8

Relaxing in the Lord. That's what these verses teach. When you feel safe and secure you don't have to worry about anything. You know that someone is taking care of you and that everything will work out just fine.

If you're going to feel that way about anyone, it should be the Lord. He's watching over your life. That means He knows everything you do. Nothing surprises Him.

So, relax in Him and let Him direct you into the person He wants you to be.

Dear Lord, I want to be able to trust You with everything. Help me learn to know that everything that happens to me is under Your control. Amen.

Work at It

Therefore, my dear brothers, stand firm. Let nothing move you. Always give yourselves fully to the work of the Lord, because you know that your labor in the Lord is not in vain.

1 Corinthians 15:58

An Olympic level gymnast doesn't just practice ten minutes a day. A concert pianist sits down and tickles the ivory more often than once or twice a week. To get really good at something, you have to give yourself to it – devote your life to it.

Becoming the person God desires for you to be is a full-time job. Full time in the sense that you spend time with Him every day and you think about what He wants for you.

Keep working for Him and learning from Him. Don't let anything move you away from that!

Dear Lord, I do want my life to count for You. Help me push other things aside and be devoted to You. Amen.

Wait - It's Worth It!

Keep yourself pure.

1 Timothy 5:22

We live in a loose society. Some people think you're totally weird if you don't have a boyfriend. But the Bible teaches you to keep yourself pure. Rather wait for the right guy before you start dating left and right. Don't give in to peer pressure just because you want to be accepted and liked.

Likewise, it is good and honorable to wait for a new outfit, book, pair of shoes. This makes us appreciate things more. Waiting and saving for something teaches us patience and appreciation.

Dear Lord, help me to remember that waiting for something is more worthwhile than getting what I want right now. Amen.

A New You

Do not lie to each other, since you have taken off your old self with its practices and have put on the new self, which is being renewed.

Colossians 3:9-10

Hey … you're a new person. You received a new heart when you asked Jesus to come into your life. You're working with new equipment here so you have a chance to see new results and become a better you.

You're going to have to make some choices though. Satan is going to keep pounding away at you, trying to make you live the way you used to. Don't let him!

Choose to keep your new heart activated so you don't lie to others and you don't keep doing the things you used to do … the things that do not please God.

Dear Lord, help me to live like a new person and to stop doing the things I used to do. I don't have to do those things anymore. I want to please You. Amen.

100

Words and Reactions

A gentle answer turns away wrath,
but a harsh word stirs up anger.

Proverbs 15:1

It's so nice on a cold night to sit in front of the fireplace and enjoy a warm fire. When the flames begin to die down and you take the poker and stir them up a bit, maybe toss another long on the fire, what happens? The flames shoot back up and burn strong, right?

Did you know that your words and reactions have that same kind of power? When there is a conflict with a family member or friend, a kind, gentle answer can keep the flames of anger from shooting up. But if you start yipping at the other person with harsh words the flames will shoot up strong ... and probably burn for a while.

Keep your responses gentle and you'll keep the flames away.

Dear Lord, please help me control my reactions and my words. Guess I'm kind of a word fireman, huh? Amen.

A Jesus Attitude

Your attitude should be the same as that of Christ Jesus ... Who made Himself nothing, taking the very nature of a servant.

Philippians 2:5, 7

Some people need to be in charge ... control freaks. They want to be the most important, make all the decisions, and not do any dirty work. Yeah, some jobs are just below them.

Well, if you have that kind of attitude you're not reflecting Christ. Does this make sense – Jesus is the Son of God ... the Creator of the universe. But He didn't have to be the most important guy in the crowd. He came to serve others. He even washed His disciples' feet. That's about the lowest job He could have done. But He wanted to meet other people's needs and do whatever He could for them.

That's the way He wants you to be, too.

Dear Lord, serving others is not what I want to do. Please help me to have an attitude like Jesus. Amen.

Be Careful What You Say

Let your conversation be always full of grace, seasoned with salt, so that you may know how to answer everyone.

Colossians 4:6

Do you know the old saying, "Sticks and stones may break my bones, but words can never hurt me"? Yeah, it's not true. Words do hurt. Unkind words just lay inside a person like a ten pound pancake.

The way you talk to others shows what's in your heart. Your words should show what makes you different from people who don't know Christ.

Let your words be filled with grace and kindness. Don't hurt others by what you say – even if you're just joking around. Sometimes your efforts to make your friends laugh are at the expense of another person.

Dear Lord, I like to make my friends laugh. But I don't want to do it by making fun of someone else or hurting anyone. Help me to be careful what I say. Amen.

No-whine Zone

Do everything without complaining or arguing, so that you ... shine like stars in the universe.

Philippians 2:14-15

Okay, you've asked Jesus to come into your life and you're doing pretty good at having devotions, praying, attending church and youth group. It looks like things are going pretty well. But – how are you doing in the no complaining or arguing category?

Complaining comes so natural to some people – whining about other people; about jobs you are told to do; about responsibilities; about lack of freedom. And arguing, well, family relationships and friendships are nearly impossible without some arguing. But, what's going to make you stand out from others – shine like a star – is if you *don't* do those things. That shows that Christ is in your life!

Dear Lord, complaining and arguing come so natural to me. Please help me with this. Amen.

Rotten Bones

A heart at peace gives life to the body,
but envy rots the bones.

Proverbs 14:30

Wanting what someone else has only leads to trouble. If you let your thoughts linger on that "want," pretty soon it's all you can think about. You want your friend's clothes, house, "stuff," talents, maybe even her parents and before you know it, your friendship with her is shot.

Envy destroys everything around it. It seeps into all your attitudes. It wrecks friendships and relationships with your own family or friends – anyone you feel may be holding you back from having what you want.

Don't let envy take control of your mind, after all, who wants rotten bones? Be at peace with what you have and who you are!

Dear God, this is hard. There is stuff I want but don't have. There are even some talents I wish I had. Help me to be content with who I am and what I have. Amen.

Heart Focus

"Where your treasure is, there your heart will be also."

Matthew 6:21

What's the most important thing in your life right now? Friends? Music? Sports? Are you not sure how to answer that question? Well, on what do you spend most of your time and energy? Bingo! That's where your treasure is.

You may think that your heart is focused on one thing – knowing and serving God or even your family – but if your time doesn't go to that, then you're just fooling yourself.

What does it mean that your heart is in the same place as your treasure? Well, think about it. Whatever your time and thoughts are focused on is quickly going to become the most important thing in your life. That means your heart is focused on it, too. Make sure your heart is focused on something worthwhile!

Dear Lord, the most worthwhile thing I can think of is You. Help me to focus on You! Amen.

We Need Each Other

Encourage one another daily.

Hebrews 3:13

People need each other. God created us to live in community with others; so we need other people around us. You know that sometimes life is hard and you get tired and discouraged. It means a lot when a friend comes along beside you with a word of encouragement. That kind word may be what keeps you going for another few days. You can be an encourager for other people, too. Pay attention to those around you. When you see someone who needs encouragement or just needs a friend, be there for her!

Take time to encourage others every day. Sometimes it's a friend, sometimes a family member who will need your encouragement. Help anyone who is struggling. You'll have the joy of helping someone you love or of making a new friend!

Dear Lord, help me pay attention to those around me. Help me be there for anyone who may need my help. Amen.

Peacefulness

Turn from evil and do good;
seek peace and pursue it.

Psalm 34:14

What kind of image does the word *peace* bring into your mind? A big field of tall grass gently blowing in the breeze? Maybe a tiny baby quietly sleeping? How about a beautiful scene of the sun setting behind a smooth lake?

Images of peace don't often include a herd of horses galloping down the road or a stock car race. What does personal peace look like, or more realistically, what does it feel like? Quiet, trusting, with no anxiety and no fear.

God wants His children to pursue that kind of peace – look for it and try to make it a part of your life. Peace like that sets God's children apart from the rest of the world.

Dear Lord, I think it must be important that this verse says to turn away from evil before looking for peace. Guess evil and peace don't go together. Help me to do good and seek peace. Amen.

Life Lessons

Teach me Your ways so I may know
You and continue to find favor with You.

Exodus 33:13

Why do teachers have to give us so much homework? It really gets old, doesn't it? Of course the reason you have homework is to help you learn – it works even if you don't think so. Well, if you want to learn to become a better person, it makes sense that you will have to let God teach you.

Sometimes lessons are hard, but they are helping you learn how to live with other people and be kind and loving.

God's lessons help you learn how to obey Him and serve Him. God's lessons, your homework, is to read His Word and talk to Him.

Dear God, I do want to learn new things so I guess if I have to do homework, I will. Help me learn quickly. Amen.

Road Maps

Ask where the good way is, and walk in it,
and you will find rest for your souls.

Jeremiah 6:16

There's an old joke that says that men will always absolutely refuse to ask directions, no matter how lost they are. Of course, it isn't fair, but there is a lesson in this. If you don't know where you're going, you can wander around in circles for a long, long time without ever getting to where you want to go. You waste a lot of time that way. You don't want to do that in your life.

But how do you find out where you should be going? You need a life map with the roads clearly marked.

Ask God to show you. He will – then, read His Word for further directions.

Most importantly, when you know which way to go – do it!

Dear Lord, help me to find the right way and to follow it closely! Amen.

Waiting Patiently

Wait for the LORD; be strong and
take heart and wait for the LORD.

Psalm 27:14

Waiting is one of the hardest things in the world. Waiting to grow up, waiting to drive, waiting to date, waiting for your dreams to come true. You can learn a lot of lessons while you're waiting though.

If you don't rush ahead into life, but wait for God to teach you and show you what He wants for you, you might be surprised at what you learn. You'll only hear His quiet voice in your heart when you're still.

Rushing around like crazy will definitely cut into your learning. God won't *make* you sit down and wait to hear His voice. He wants it to be your choice.

Dear God, it's hard to sit down and just be still. There is always something to do. Help me learn to be still before You. Amen.

Good Forgiveness

Bear with each other and forgive whatever grievances you may have against one another. Forgive as the Lord forgave you.

Colossians 3:13

You're not going to get anywhere in your Christian life if you don't learn to forgive others. After all, God has forgiven you for the wrong things you've done – learn from that and be willing to forgive others.

Being able to forgive, even really mean things, will show that you have God's love in you.

Forgiving isn't easy – it's easier to be angry or hold a grudge. But you can be better than that. When you're angry with someone, forgiving them shows how far you've come in your walk with God. It is the best you possible!

Dear God, help me be more forgiving. Help me remember how often You forgive me for the things I do. Amen.

Be Like Christ

The wisdom that comes from heaven is first of all pure; then peace-loving, considerate, submissive, full of mercy and good fruit, impartial and sincere.

James 3:17

If you keep on doing what you do, you'll continue to get what you got. For example, if you eat junk food all the time, you're gonna be overweight. If you read comic books non-stop, you'll never learn your school lessons.

In the same way, change what you put into your mind if you want to have different actions come out. What you put in your mind and heart will become visible in how you live and how you treat others.

Make good choices, spend time in God's Word, ask God to teach you with His wisdom. Seek to become that kind, considerate person who shows God's love to everyone around her. Stand out from the crowd – be more Christlike.

Dear Lord, I do want to be more like Christ. Teach me. Please show me how! Amen.

Loving Others

Whoever loves his brother lives in the light,
and there is nothing in him to make him stumble.

1 John 2:10

One command that's given over and over in the Bible is "Love one another." When you're around friends who like to talk about other people, it's a real temptation to join right in with them. It can get to be such a habit that you don't even realize you're doing it. That is NOT showing love.

Another thing that happens is that your group can become so close that other girls aren't accepted. They're always left on the outside – a lonely place to be.

Becoming the young woman God wants you to be will mean that you are loving to all those around you. That will set you apart from others.

Dear Lord, I've never thought about how other kids might feel if they're not accepted into my group of friends. Help me to be loving and to encourage my friends to be loving, too. Amen.

Differences

Do not curse the deaf or put a stumbling block in front of the blind, but fear your God. I am the LORD.

Leviticus 19:14

How do you feel about kids who are "different" from you? Do deaf or blind people make you uncomfortable? How about kids in wheelchairs – especially those who have diseases that make it difficult for them to speak or control their hand movements.

Yeah, they are different, but that doesn't give you the right to give them a hard time or make fun of them ... or ignore them.

Take the time to get to know someone who is different. You might discover a really wonderful person. And you might give a lonely person the gift of friendship!

Dear God, some people kind of scare me. But, I want to get past that. Give me the courage to start a conversation with someone who is different from me. Amen.

All Are Gifted

We have different gifts, according to the grace given us.

Romans 12:6

"I wish I could play the piano like Sarah does." "I wish I could do gymnastics like Mallory." "I wish I had straight blond hair like Cori." "Why can't I talk with new people like Joy does?"

Are you always comparing yourself to other girls ... and feeling as if you come up short? Well ... *stop it*. God gave each person different gifts, and He gave *all* of us gifts. We're all different, but we all need to work together to make God's family the best it can be. Don't wish your life away by wanting the gifts someone else has.

Ask God to show you what gifts He has given you – what you're good at and what you enjoy. Then go to work developing those gifts to become the best you possible!

Dear Lord, show me what my gifts are. Help me learn to use them every day – for You! Amen.

Get Excited

Never be lacking in zeal, but keep
your spiritual fervor, serving the Lord.

Romans 12:11

Zeal ... that's not a word you hear a lot anymore. What does it mean? Energy, enthusiasm, passion. In other words – you feel zeal for things you are really excited about. Is there anything in your life that you have zeal for? Not just zeal for a minute or two, but real zeal that consumes your thoughts and energy? Maybe you aren't zealous about anything right now.

Well, God doesn't want any of His children to be lukewarm about their faith or about serving Him. He wants your zeal! Get excited about what God has done for you. Get excited about how much He loves you. Get excited about His plans for your life.

Don't let anything spoil your excitement.

Dear God, I didn't even know what zeal meant before this. But I want to have zeal for You! Help me to get excited about You! Amen.

The Best Life Ever

For to me, to live is Christ and to die is gain.

Philippians 1:21

Pretty serious verse. What's it saying? That the most important thing in living is to glorify Christ. What does that mean? Glorifying Christ is when everything in your life points to Him.

It's done by obeying God – living by the standards of His Word. It's done by giving Him credit for your life and by recognizing His creative power.

What does the second part of this verse mean – dying is gain? It means that heaven is God's gift to His children. Heaven is a more wonderful place than can ever be imagined! There's no sadness, no sin, no problems, just wonderful time with God.

Knowing that heaven is in your future is awesome!

Dear God, making Jesus the focus of my life and living for Him every day ... well, I have a ways to go. Please help me. Amen.

Don't Toot Your Own Horn

Clothe yourselves with humility toward one another, because, "God opposes the proud but gives grace to the humble."

1 Peter 5:5

Everyone knows one. Every crowd has one – that one person who brags about everything she does. That one person who thinks she is better, smarter, prettier and just plain old more important than anyone else. Those kind of people aren't much fun to be around, are they? Truth is, they don't please God much either. He's more kind toward humble people. People who lift up others, encouraging them to be the best people they can be.

Braggy people lift themselves up by pushing other people down. That stinks. Don't toot your own horn – if you do, then your song may not be worth playing.

Dear God, help me remember this every time I'm tempted to brag about myself. Help me to see the good things in other people and to encourage them. Amen.

Hopefulness

Put your hope in God, for I will yet
praise Him, my Savior and my God.

Psalm 42:5

Where's your hope? Your hope – what you think will pull you through when the going gets tough.There are so many things in this world that claim to be worthy of your hope. But are they? Friends are good, wonderful even, but are they worthy of putting your hope in?

Popularity, money, success, fame, these are all things that claim they are worthy of your hope. But, are they?

Would those things actually be able to help you in a crisis? Are they worth giving all your time and energy to? No way!

The only person worthy of your hope is God! Be different from the world. Put your hope in God only. Live for Him and praise Him!

Dear God, thank You for loving me. Thank You for all You give me. I praise You with all my heart. Amen.

Truth First

Do not deceive one another.

Leviticus 19:11

"You're my best friend." When you hear those words from someone you really care about, then find out that she didn't mean it at all ... well, it hurts.

No one likes to be lied to. Not even those little white lies like "Yeah, your hair looks good that way" when it really looks like a floor mop gone wild.

Lies hurt. Becoming the best person you can be means stopping the lies. Don't even say the "I-don't-want-to-hurt-your-feelings-so-I'm-just-gonna-fudge-a-little" kind of lies.

It is possible to be honest and kind at the same time. Show enough respect for your family and friends to tell them the truth. Always.

Dear God, I hate it when someone lies to me. I don't want to hurt my friends that way. Help me always tell the truth and to find a kind way to do that. Amen.

To Sum It Up!

Let love and faithfulness never leave you;
bind them around your neck, write them
on the tablet of your heart.

Proverbs 3:3

What have you learned about becoming the best you ever? There's two pretty basic foundations to that happening. Number one is to love God and love others. God's Word says over and over to love Him and love others. It says it a lot, so it must be important.

The second thing is to trust God. Believe who He is and what He has done for you. You can't really love Him if you don't trust Him. You can't live your life for Him if you don't love Him. There's a chain reaction here.

Now, how do you grow more in love with God and learn to trust Him more? Simple ... read His Word. Talk with Him. Ask Him for His Spirit's help.

Dear God, You want me to be the best person I can be. That's why I know You will help me. Let's get going! Amen.

Praises Ring!

The LORD is my strength and my song; He has become my salvation. He is my God, and I will praise Him, my father's God, and I will exalt Him.

Exodus 15:2

Have you ever gone to a high school football or basketball game? Did you enjoy watching the cheerleaders who try to get the crowd excited about the game by leading cheers? They do amazing routines, sometimes even tossing one another into the air. Their energy and enthusiasm is contagious. Praising God is like being a cheerleader for Him.

Moses' words of praise are recorded in Exodus and he couldn't say enough good things about God! Praising God can be done privately and publicly. Praising God means recognizing all the wonderful things He is and does!

Dear God, I want to praise You, too! Thank You for putting prayers like this one in the Bible so I can see how others have praised You through the years! Amen.

Thanks for the Good Times

Is any one of you in trouble? He should pray.
Is anyone happy? Let him sing songs of praise.

James 5:13

Sometimes life doesn't work out the way you planned – there are those times when it seems like absolutely *nothing* is going right. When most people have trouble in their lives they cry out to God for help. People expect God to do something for them when they have a crisis. They are also ready to blame Him for some of the problems.

But, when things are going well, do those same people remember to praise God for His gifts and for the good times in their lives? Mmm – sometimes, but not nearly enough.

Remember to turn to God for help when you need it. He wants to help you. But don't forget to praise Him when things are going well! He also wants to know that you appreciate His care.

Dear God, thank You for the good times in my life. They make the hard times easier to handle. Amen.

Hope Equals Praise

Now there is in store for me the crown of righteousness,
which the Lord, the righteous Judge, will award
to me on that day – and not only to me,
but also to all who have longed for His appearing.

2 Timothy 4:8

God promises hope – a crown of righteousness – that's in heaven! You see, even if you have spent most of your life just doing your own thing and not caring a bit about what God wants – even if you have deliberately disobeyed God and turned your back on Him – you can have hope.

That's 'cause God looks at your heart, and He sees if you have a longing for Him, a longing for Christ to come back, a longing to obey and please God. He sees what your real desires are and He gives you a chance to change.

Dear God, thank You for looking at my heart instead of at the stupid things I do all the time. I do want to obey You and I praise You for giving me chance after chance! Amen.

Praise God for Creation!

God saw all that He had made, and it was very good.

Genesis 1:31

God spent six busy days making everything there is on this earth ... including the earth itself. He's the reason you have anything to enjoy, anything to do, anyone to love. All He had to do was say a word and things started happening. Nothing that God made was by accident. He thought about what He was making and after He made it all, He looked at it and decided He had done a good job. Things turned out the way He wanted.

Praise God for thinking of everything in this world. Praise Him for caring about what you would enjoy. Praise Him for paying attention to detail. Praise Him for making this great big wonderful world!

Dear God, sometimes I take Your creation for granted. I am thankful for this world. It's beautiful. You did a great job! Amen.

White as Snow

"Though your sins are like scarlet, they shall be as white as snow; though they are red as crimson, they shall be like wool."

Isaiah 1:18

If you've ever spilled spaghetti sauce on a white sweater you know that a red stain is hard to get out. You can scrub and scrub and use all kinds of special treatments, but it's very *hard* to get rid of the spot. Even when you've washed it over and over and no one else can see the stain – you still can 'cause you know where it is.

Well, that's kind of how your sins are to God's pureness. Like a bright red stain that only fades to pink. But Jesus' death on the cross took care of the stain. Because of Him your sins are *gone* – you look white as snow now! Praise God for that!

Dear God, wow! Thank You so much. What a wonderful plan to get rid of the sin stain on my heart. You're awesome! Amen.

Heart-felt Praise

I will praise You, O LORD, with all my heart;
I will tell of all Your wonders.

Psalm 9:1

Praise cannot be half-hearted. It's not one of those things that you can "sort of" do. The psalmist knew that and he committed to praising God with all his heart. He even told God how he would praise Him – by telling about all of God's wonders. That could be things like how a bird flies, how a butterfly begins life as a caterpillar, or why the ocean stays within the boundaries God made for it.

You might tell of the wonder that God loves you, not only you, but all the people who ever lived. Maybe the wonder that fascinates you is the hope of being in heaven for eternity! Whatever it is, praise God loud and clear for it.

Dear God, it's good to stop and think about Your wonders and which of them is most important to me! I thank You and praise You for them all. Amen.

Focus

My eyes are ever on the LORD.

Psalm 25:15

When you start learning to drive you'll find out that more often than not, wherever you're looking is where the car will be going. Where your focus is plays a big role in where you go.

Of course, when you're driving that's good motivation for keeping your eyes on the road – otherwise your teacher will scream a lot!

This carries through to your Christian life. As long as you keep your eyes firmly on God, you'll be fine. But, if you let your eyes wander to other things – popularity, boys, fashion, even self-centeredness – anything that pulls you away from God, well, you're gonna have trouble.

Dear God, I praise You for helping me all the time! Help me keep my eyes on You. I want to stay focused and not be tempted to put too much importance on the wrong things. Amen.

Always the Same

Jesus Christ is the same yesterday
and today and forever.

Hebrews 13:8

There are a million things to praise God for. One major thing, though, would be His constancy. What does that mean? It means that Jesus is never in a bad mood. He's never out to make you look bad while He looks good.

You know when you go to Him in prayer that He is going to be exactly the same today as He was yesterday and will be tomorrow.

Jesus' purpose is to help you know God and grow closer and closer to Him. You'll always get what you expect when you go to God.

Dear God, there's a lot of comfort in that. I know that You always love me, always consider certain things sin and are pleased with other things … always. Amen.

He Hears, Cares and Acts

I sought the LORD, and He answered me;
He delivered me from all my fears.

Psalm 34:4

"My hero!" That's what the damsels in distress would say to their rescuers in the old movies. When someone saves you from danger he becomes your hero and you shower him with thanks and usually tell others about his good deeds.

Have you turned to God when you were afraid and later realized that He helped you through the difficult situation?

Did you realize that He not only helped you – He heard your prayer and cared about what you were facing? That's certainly something to praise God for. He hears. He cares. He acts. Praise God!

Dear Father, I am so thankful that You hear my prayers and that You answer them. Thank You! Amen.

The Cavalry Rides In!

Guard the good deposit that was entrusted to you – guard it with the help of the Holy Spirit who lives in us.

2 Timothy 1:14

A familiar scene in old movies would be when the good guys are outnumbered by the bad guys. The battle is raging on and it looks pretty hopeless for the good guys. But, suddenly, the cavalry rides in! They fight off the bad guys and save the day for the good guys!

Ah ... if only life were like the movies. Well, maybe it is! You don't have to fight off the bad guy by yourself, either. Here's the scoop – when you gave your life to Jesus, you became His child and He will help you guard your heart. The Holy Spirit will ride over the hill and fight off whoever and whatever is threatening you – just call on Him! Praise God for the cavalry!

Dear God, it's awesome to know that I'm not alone. Thanks for the Holy Spirit and all His help. Amen.

Amazing Forgiveness!

You are a forgiving God, gracious and compassionate, slow to anger and abounding in love.

Nehemiah 9:17

Praise God for His forgiveness. That's something He has to do over and over for most of us. Stop and think about how hurt and angry you feel toward a friend who hurts your feelings – especially if it was on purpose! It's hard to forgive – especially more than once! Really think about the act of forgiving. It's hard, isn't it?

Now, do you realize how incredible it is that God is willing to forgive you over and over and over! He loves you that much!

Take time to thank Him ... not just thank Him ... but praise Him for His forgiveness!

Dear God, I don't deserve it. You forgive my mistakes and my selfish acts over and over. I just don't deserve it. But I sure am thankful! Amen.

Close to You

The LORD is near to all who call
on Him, to all who call on Him in truth.

Psalm 145:18

Movie stars, athletes, politicians all travel with an entourage. That means it's nearly impossible to get close to them. If you wait for hours in a crowd to see your favorite singer, you'll probably have to look through a crowd of bodyguards to get a glimpse of her.

Seems that if famous people are that hard to get close to, then it would be nearly impossible to get close to God – the Creator of *everything*. Well, praise Him 'cause that's not true!

It is so amazing – God, the Creator of the universe; God who hears the prayers of all mankind; God who deals with all kinds of natural disasters and really *serious* stuff is near to little ole you. He loves you.

Dear God, every time I think about it I'm amazed that even with all the major stuff You have to take care of, You care about me too. Thank You. Amen.

Light in Darkness

God is light; in Him there is no darkness at all.

1 John 1:5

Have you ever tried to find your way through a room when it is dark; so dark that you can't even see your own hand in front of your face? Pretty scary, huh? Trying to walk when you can't tell if there is something solid to put your foot on is unnerving.

Growing up feels like that sometimes. There are so many choices to make about what kind of person you're going to be and what are the right things to do. The options pulling at you make it feel like you're walking in total darkness and the right path is lost.

The Hope – the Light – is God. Seek Him and the right path will light up for you. Maybe not as bright as an airport runway, but you will be able to see it in the darkness.

Dear Lord, I praise You for being the Light. Your light helps me find my way in the dark times of life. Amen.

Amazing Love

"As the Father has loved Me, so have I loved you."

John 15:9

Ahhh, sweet love. Girls tend to get all mushy thinking about love. Be honest now, is there some guy that you spend time daydreaming about? Thinking about how it would be to know that he loved you? Everyone wants to be loved. Everyone wants to know they are special to someone. There's nothing wrong with that. But, in the middle of that daydreaming, don't forget that there is already Someone who loves you more than you can imagine (Someone besides your family).

The words from John 15 were spoken by Jesus. Think about what He's saying – in the same way that His Father loves Him, He loves you! That's complete, total, no-holds-barred love! Love that watches out for you, cares about you, will never, never fade away. Amazing!

Dear God, it's hard to comprehend that You love me that much! I'm so thankful You do. I praise You for Your amazing love! Amen.

Love in Action

He poured water into a basin and began to wash His disciples' feet, drying them with the towel that was wrapped around Him.

John 13:5

Jesus didn't just teach with words. He also taught by example. He wanted His disciples to understand how important it is to do things for others that aren't easy; things that some people think they're too good to do. Washing feet was a job that servants usually did. It was something that one of His disciples should have done for Him ... but none of them did.

God put stories like this in the Bible to show that sometimes it's important to get your hands dirty and do the jobs that no one else wants to do. Do something for someone else that shows them how important they are to you. Follow Jesus' example and remember to praise Him for being that example!

Dear God, I do praise You for examples like this. Please help me, I will try my best to follow Your example. Amen.

Reach Out and Touch

Filled with compassion, Jesus reached out His hand and touched the man.

Mark 1:41

"Reach out and touch someone" used to be the advertising slogan of a big telephone company. People long to be touched. The human touch conveys love and acceptance – no matter how distasteful a person might be. A man with leprosy came to Jesus asking to be healed.

Leprosy is a highly contagious disease and is spread through touching the sores of a leper. In Jesus' day, having leprosy meant you were pushed out of society. Lepers had to live away from their families and NO ONE wanted to touch them. Jesus could have healed the man with just a word or even a thought. He didn't have to touch him, but He did. Praise God that He cares enough to reach out and touch you. That's real love!

Dear God, thanks for loving me that much. What Jesus did helps me know that You'll never turn away from me. Amen.

He Cares

When the Lord saw her, His heart went out to her and He said, "Don't cry."

Luke 7:13

It might be easy to think that God is so busy with the "big" stuff of this world that He doesn't really have time to care about the things that weigh down our hearts. But, that's just not true. God cares when your heart is hurting.

Jesus met a woman who was a widow – the only family she had left in the world was her son who had just died. She was on her way to bury the boy when Jesus met her.

Read the verse again – His heart went out to her. Jesus cared about her pain. If He cared about her pain, you can know that He cares about yours, too! Praise Him for caring when your heart hurts!

Dear God, I am thankful for Your care. It is amazing to know that You care when my heart is hurting! Amen.

No Excuses

"Ask and it will be given to you; seek and you will find; knock and the door will be opened to you."

Luke 11:9

You try to tell your teacher, "Uhhh, I didn't know there was gonna be a test." Nope, won't work 'cause she knows that means you didn't pay attention. You can tell your parents, "Uhhh, I didn't know I was supposed to clean my room." Nope, won't work either 'cause you're not new to the house rules.

You can even try telling God, "Uhhh, I didn't know You'd help me." Nope, won't work 'cause here's the promise that He will. All you have to do is ask and He will give you what you need. Look for Him and you will find Him.

Do you get it – He *wants* to help you, but He wants you to ask Him for His help. How awesome is that? God Himself wants you to ask Him for help!

Dear God, thank You, thank You, thank You. It's amazing that You love me that much! Amen.

The Most Wonderful Gift

He saved us, not because of righteous things we had done, but because of His mercy.

Titus 3:5

Think you're pretty cool, do ya? Think you've got your act together and you're in the "coolest" group? Think you're just a bit better than some other kids? Well ... get over yourself. The most awesome thing that has or ever will happen to you, you had absolutely nothing to do with.

The highest status you could achieve is being a member of God's family. That happened when you were saved – and being saved is something you definitely did not deserve.

God saved you just because He loves you, not because you earned it. Praise Him for your salvation – the most wonderful gift that was completely undeserved.

Dear Father, I am so thankful for Your awesome salvation. You're amazing! Amen.

Handmade

For we are God's workmanship, created
in Christ Jesus to do good works,
which God prepared in advance for us to do.

Ephesians 2:10

Have you ever worked very hard to make something? Maybe you made some pottery, painted a picture, wrote a story ... whatever it was ... you were incredibly proud and protective of it, right? You wanted others to respect it and be careful with it.

Well, put yourself right there in that category. You are God's workmanship. He created you and He is very protective of you. He wants others ... and you, yourself, to be careful with you.

You were created with a purpose in mind. How awesome is that? You can do something for God – a job He planned just for you.

Dear God, it is totally amazing that You made me and You are proud of what You made! It is also very exciting that there is a job I can do for You! Amen.

A New You

Therefore, if anyone is in Christ, he is
a new creation; the old has gone, the new has come.

2 Corinthians 5:17

Okay, this is pretty gross, but did you know that snakes shed their skins and grow new ones? Yeah, they just crawl right out of the old ones and within a few days they have new skin. How cool is that?

Can you crawl out of your skin? You kind of can. When you asked Jesus into your life, He made you brand new. The old you – the one that doesn't pay any attention to God and just does what she wants – is gone.

In its place is the new you – the one who cares about God and wants to obey Him and live the life He wants you to live. How cool is *that*? You are a new you, because of Christ.

Dear God, that is so awesome. Thank You for making me new ... completely new! Amen.

Always Available

Praise be to the Lord, to God our Savior,
who daily bears our burdens.

Psalm 68:19

When you need extra math help from your teacher, do you have to make an appointment to see her? You can't just drop in at her house on a Sunday afternoon, right? What about a dentist appointment? You've got a terrible toothache but you can't see your dentist until a week from Tuesday ... bummer.

Here's something cool – you don't have to make an appointment to meet with God. He doesn't have strict office hours between 9 and 5. He's available to you every single day, in fact, every moment of every day and night. He's there to help you with your problems, in fact to lift them off your shoulders and take care of them for you.

Dear Lord, I'm so thankful that I can come to You any time of the day or night and know that You're there. Thank You so much. Amen.

Unchanging Love

So we know and rely
on the love God has for us.

1 John 4:16

There are not many absolutely sure things in this world, things that you can trust all the time. Friends fail you once in a while and stuff certainly breaks down.

The one thing you can count on every single time is God's love for you. When everything else falls away; when you're feeling totally and completely alone, you can count on the fact that God is there … loving you just like always. His constant love is a foundation that you can build the rest of your life on.

Praise Him for His love; His constant, pure, unfailing love. Love that never changes. You can always count on that.

Dear God, I do praise You for Your love. I know I'm not always easy to love, but You do it. Thanks. Amen.

Strength and Peace

The LORD gives strength to His people;
the LORD blesses His people with peace.

Psalm 29:11

"It's too hard. I can't do it!" Ever said that? About what? Math, gym class, being nice to someone who was mean to you? Everyone faces hard things – different things for everyone – but hard none the less.

Did you know you have a secret weapon you can call on? A secret weapon? Yes – *God*. You don't have to face hard stuff alone. God's strength that created the universe, parted the waters of the Red Sea and raised Jesus back to life – that's the strength available to you. All you have to do is ask Him. He's waiting to help you. Of course, when you have that strength in your life, peace comes right along with it.

Dear Lord, thank You for Your strength and peace. I'm so thankful that You are in my life. Amen.

An Example to Follow

Christ suffered for you, leaving you an example, that you should follow in His steps.

1 Peter 2:21

Things are easier to do if you have an example to follow. When you're making a new recipe, it's easier if there are pictures. When you're learning a new game, instructions help. If you're learning a new trick in gymnastics, having someone show it to you helps a lot.

Living the Christian life – the way God wants you to live it – can be kind of confusing. So, it helps that you have an example to follow. Jesus walked on this earth, had choices to make, was tempted, had to deal with difficult people, had to choose to have prayer time – all the things you have to deal with. He left an example to follow. Be like Jesus and life will be much easier.

Dear Father, thank You for Jesus' example. It helps a lot to have someone to follow. Amen.

Your Bodyguard

"When you pass through the waters, I will be with you; and when you pass through the rivers, they will not sweep over you. When you walk through the fire, you will not be burned … for I am the Lord, your God."

Isaiah 43:2-3

Praise God for watching out for you! Absolutely nothing surprises Him. He knows every tough thing you have ever faced – or ever will. If your family is breaking up because your parents fight all the time – He knows. If someone you love is dying – He knows. If you're lonely – He knows.

Get this: *You are not alone*. He's with you in all those difficult situations and as tough as they are to go through, they won't kill you. He's your God and He's watching out for you. Hold tight to Him and praise Him for being with you.

Dear God, sometimes I'm scared. Sometimes I feel alone. Thank You for reminding me that You are with me and watching out for me always. Amen.

Praise Him!

"The people I formed for Myself
that they may proclaim My praise."

Isaiah 43:21

God gives you so much – everything. He created this earth for you to live on and the sun to warm it. He filled the night sky with beautiful stars. He made oceans, mountains, rivers, flowers. He created butterflies and puppies and kittens and ponies. He made families to love you and care for you. He gave you friends to fill your life with laughter.

What other things can you add to this list? What is your response to all God has given you? He wants it to be praise for Him.

Celebrate His goodness and love by telling others about Him. Praise Him!

Dear Father, I praise You for Your wonderful gifts. I praise You for Your care for me. I praise You for who You are! Amen.

Patience

He is patient with you, not wanting anyone
to perish, but everyone to come to repentance.

2 Peter 3:9

Team try-outs can be so stressful. If you've ever tried out for a sports team, dance team or cheerleading squad you know how stressful it is. They have a certain number of slots to fill and everyone who tries out will not make the team. Truthfully, the coaches don't want everyone on the team. They want only those they consider to be the best.

Thank God that He isn't that way. He wants everyone to be part of His family. Praise Him for His patience – He's waiting for more and more people to come to Him. He wants everyone to be able to spend eternity with Him in heaven.

Dear Father, I'm so thankful that You waited for me. I'm thankful that my family and friends who don't know You still have a chance to choose You! Amen.

Everlasting Love

This is how God showed His love among us:
He sent His one and only Son into
the world that we might live through Him.

1 John 4:9

The easy way to "show love" is to drop a few dollars into a jar to help victims of some disaster begin to rebuild their lives. Or, if you know someone who lost a job and is having a tough time paying their bills, money helps.

But there is another, more personal way to show love and it is what God did for you. He gave you His most precious Son – His only Son. God certainly could have come up with a plan to save the world without giving up His Son. But, He wanted us to *know* how *much* He loves us. Therefore He gave the One He loves the most.

Dear God, I know You sent Jesus, but I never thought about how much love that shows me. Thank You for loving me so much! Amen.

He Understands

Jesus ... was led by the Spirit in the desert,
where for forty days He was tempted by the devil.

Luke 4:1-2

Quit complaining about how tough your life is and how no one understands what you're dealing with. Jesus does. He spent forty days with Satan bombarding Him with temptation after temptation. He didn't eat or drink for that whole time. He was tired and weak and Satan never left Him alone.

He knows what temptation feels like. He knows that when you're tired, it's hard to fight it off. You can trust Him to help you, because He knows what you're going through. Praise God for this plan. It means that Jesus can identify with your struggles. He can help because He understands.

Dear God, I'm sure it was hard to let Jesus go through that – but thank You. It makes a difference that Jesus understands. Amen.

152

Always, in All Ways!

Let them praise the name of the LORD,
for His name alone is exalted; His
splendor is above the earth and the heavens.

Psalm 148:13

Get serious about praising God. Psalm 148 talks about all of creation praising Him. The oceans, skies, mountains and creatures all praise Him. Be honest with yourself now, how much time do you spend talking about your favorite band or movie star? How much of your conversation is about a cute boy?

God alone is worthy of your praise. Let Him hear it. Sing out your praises for His love, power, care, forgiveness and protection. Praise Him by the way you live your life. Praise Him to others. Praise Him always in all ways!

Dear Father, I spend more time asking You for stuff than praising You. I'm sorry. I praise You for all You are and all You do! Amen.

Number One!

"Love the Lord your God with all your heart and with all your soul and with all your mind. This is the first and greatest commandment."

Matthew 22:37-38

Do you ever wonder what is *really* important in life? After all, there are so many things thrown at you – especially from advertisers."Get skinny!" "Wear this kind of jeans!" "Listen to this music!" Put things in perspective. Whatever you have been treating as the most important thing in the world is probably not.

It may be hard for you to believe that anything could be more important than what your friends think or being popular. But, these verses lay out that – nothing should be more important to you than loving God completely. No one is saying that friends aren't important, but keep them in perspective. When you love God with all your heart, soul and mind – nothing will come before Him.

Dear God, help me to get my priorities straight. I want You to be my top priority. Amen.

Number Two Priority

This is the first and greatest commandment, and the second is like it: "Love your neighbor as yourself."

Matthew 22:38-39

When push comes to shove, most people will say that God is powerful and important. But, after God, what's in the number two spot? The Bible says number two is others.

Now, here's the weird part – loving others in the same way you love yourself.

What does that mean? Well, you take care of yourself, keep yourself safe, make yourself look good, in general, you look out for yourself. God says to do that for others, too, and not just your friends. He means even people you don't know well or people you don't especially like.

Hey, it's not easy ... but you can always ask God for help.

Dear God, I'm going to need Your help! I know some people who aren't very easy to love. Amen.

A Good Thing

It is good to praise the LORD and make music to Your name, O Most High, to proclaim Your love in the morning and Your faithfulness at night.

Psalm 92:1-2

Okay, time to be honest with yourself – do you get tired of other (older) people constantly telling you what to do? Honestly, do you sometimes feel as though you don't have the opportunity to set your own priorities because someone else is doing it for you? Yeah, it does feel like that sometimes.

But one thing you do have control over is your heart. Even if others direct your time, they can't control what your heart feels. You must choose whether or not you will praise God.

Here's a chance to make a mature choice – begin and end your days by praising God. It's a good thing to do.

Dear God, I want praise for You to be my first thought in the morning and the last one I have at night. Praise You! Amen.

Your Choice

We must pay more careful attention, therefore, to what we have heard, so that we do not drift away.

Hebrews 2:1

What kind of music do you listen to? Come on, be honest, what are the words; what does the story lift up and honor?

Okay, what kinds of movies or television shows do you watch? What's the message about lifestyles and choices? The world is bombarding you with junk ... sinful priorities.

If living for God and obeying Him is going to be a priority for you, you will have to *choose* it. Pay attention to what you learned in Sunday school and church.

Choose to spend time reading His Word, listen to music about Him, talk with Him. It's going to have to be a choice ... your choice.

Dear God, I never thought about what kind of stuff I put in my mind through music, movies and TV. I want to make You my priority. Give me strength to make that my choice. Amen.

Trust Focus

"Do not let your hearts be troubled.
Trust in God; trust also in Me."

John 14:1

Are you thinking ... "Don't let my heart be troubled? Whoever said that must be crazy." Think so? Well, then you're calling Jesus crazy. Yeah, He said this. He knew that your life would be tough sometimes.

Jesus understands people. He knew that you'd put your hope for making things better in other kids or in things. He wanted you to know that none of those things can give you peace.

Only trust in Him can settle your troubled heart. It's not easy to switch your trust focus. But, you gotta start somewhere.

Believe that God knows what's going on. Believe that He can do something to help you. Trust Him to do it.

Dear God, help me to start placing my trust in You. I already know other things don't work. I want to learn to trust You. Amen.

Always Learning

Show me Your ways, O Lord, teach me Your paths; guide me in Your truth and teach me, for You are God my Savior and my hope is in You all day long.

Psalm 25:4-5

From the first steps of a baby to the teen's independence, the world constantly changes. More freedom means more choices which calls for more teaching and guidance. You're growing up and the choices before you are more significant than they were when you were a child.

You're facing choices that range from fooling around with boys and smoking to the people you hang out with, what you think about God, how you treat other people and your opinion of yourself. The best place to go for guidance during this journey is the Lord. Ask His help. Put your hope in Him.

Dear God, seems like there is always something to learn. But I want to learn what You can teach me. Guide me, please, guide me. Amen.

Flip the Switch

May the God of peace ... equip you
with everything good for doing His will.

Hebrews 13:20-21

Think about it – you walk into a dark room, flip a switch and the room is flooded with light. The light is always there, waiting for you to use by flipping the switch.

In the same way, everything you need to live for God is right in front of you just waiting for you to access it. His instructions on how to live are in the Bible – everything you need to know to live a life of obedience.

And, if that's not enough, God is ready and waiting for you to talk with Him. He wants to guide you and show you what gifts and abilities He has given you. All you have to do is flip the switch to be equipped by Him.

Dear Father, it's pretty exciting to think that You've given me everything I need to be able to do Your will. Help me find the "switch" and flip it on. Amen.

Motive Check

You do not have, because you do not ask God.
When you ask, you do not receive,
because you ask with wrong motives, that
you may spend what you get on your pleasures.

James 4:2-3

Do your prayers have "I trouble"? Are they mostly what you want God to do for you? If so, you may need to change your style. Talking with God about stuff that's important to you is what prayer is all about. But God is not a genie in a bottle to make you gorgeous, popular and rich.

Check your motives. Are you praying for things that will spread the message of His love to others? Are you asking Him to help you live in obedience to Him?

If your prayers aren't being answered, it may be that your motives are wrong.

Dear Father, help me to examine my motives and make sure I'm asking for stuff for the right reasons. I want a powerful prayer life! Amen.

Wearing Love

The fruit of the Spirit is love.

Galatians 5:22

Are you a member of any kind of sports team or performing group? If so, you probably have a uniform to wear. When you come into a room and see someone in a uniform like yours, you know you're on the same team.

You're identifiable by your appearance. Well, that's true of a child of God, too. If you've asked Christ into your heart, His Spirit is living inside you and that will be evident by the love that flows from you.

The Spirit's love is the kind of love that gives others a chance, even if they are "different." It's a love that doesn't gossip or criticize. It's God's love and it comes from deep inside.

Are you identifiable by your love?

Dear Lord, I'm good at loving my friends, but sometimes I'm not very loving to others. Fill me with Your love so people will know I'm Your child. Amen.

Showing Joy

The fruit of the Spirit is love, joy ...

Galatians 5:22

Do you know someone who always has a problem? Someone who constantly complains about stuff? Someone who looks at life with a "glass half-empty instead of half-full" viewpoint? It isn't much fun to be always around someone who is complaining. Hopefully that isn't you.

As a child of God, who has His Spirit living in your heart, one of the identifiable characteristics of your life should be joy. After all, you know God loves you. You know His power and guidance and that He is working in your life. You know that heaven is in your future. Why shouldn't you be joyful? Even when you have problems, you don't have to be hopeless.

Are you identifiable by your joy?

Dear Lord, don't let me get stuck in a complaining rut. Let me be joyous and share joy with those around me. Amen.

Peaceful Heart

The fruit of the Spirit is love, joy, peace ...

Galatians 5:22

"I'm scared of storms." "I worry about wars." "What if my parents split up?" When you think about it, there are all kinds of things to worry about. If you let your mind wander to all the things that *could* happen, you could spend a lot of time worrying. However, a heart filled with worry is the opposite of a heart filled with peace.

One characteristic of a heart where God's Spirit lives is peace. This heart knows that God is in control of everything – nothing surprises Him. No matter how bad things seem to be in the world or in your life, you can trust Him to take care of you and those you love. He never leaves you alone.

A heart that belongs to God is identifiable by peace.

Dear Father, my life is not nearly as peaceful as I would like it to be. Help me learn to trust You more so I can be peaceful. Amen.

Patience Is a Virtue

The fruit of the Spirit is love, joy, peace, patience ...

Galatians 5:22

"Why can't I date?" "I can't wait to get a driver's license." "It will be so cool when I can go to college." "I just want to move out on my own ..." Impatience is almost a way of life these days. From the frustration of waiting in line to waiting to grow up, people try to hurry life up.

That big hurry spreads to the way people are treated, too. You may know someone that, for whatever reason, really rings your impatience bell ... someone you want to help finish sentences or help make decisions!

A heart in which God's Spirit lives is identifiable by its patience – with others and with situations. Cut others some slack and don't stress about stuff. Are you identifiable by your patience?

Dear Father, no, I'm not exactly patient. Please help me by filling me with the patience of Your Spirit. Amen.

Kind Speech

The fruit of the Spirit is love,
joy, peace, patience, kindness ...

Galatians 5:22

What's the sharpest, most dangerous item you can think of? Nope, the right answer is the tongue. Yeah, it's unreal how much the words you speak can hurt another person. Well, you've probably been on the receiving end of mean comments. You know how the bad feelings just lay on your heart making you feel bad like no one in the world could like you.

Well, your unkind words do that to others, too. A life filled with the power of God's Spirit is identifiable by kindness – that's especially noticeable by the words that are spoken. Ask God to help you think about the words you speak ... and not just the words but also the tone of your voice. Be identified by kindness!

Dear God, I know how lousy I feel when someone says something mean to me. Don't let me do that to anyone else. Help me be kind. Amen.

Sooooo Good!

The fruit of the Spirit is love, joy,
peace, patience, kindness, goodness ...

Galatians 5:22

What kinds of things are good? Chocolate? Ice cream? How about chocolate ice cream? Music? Movies? Books? Think about how many times you use the word good. Now, how often do you use this word to describe another person?

A good person is probably someone who is honest, nice, kind – a lot of good characteristics rolled into one. Just about everyone is good some of the time – but it's so hard. People can be so annoying sometimes.

Or, when a teacher has been picking on you, maybe you just want to lash out at someone. Being fair, honest and kind is sometimes far, far away from where your heart is. But when God's Holy Spirit lives inside you, goodness shows to those around you.

Dear Lord, I want people to see goodness when they look at me – Your goodness. Amen.

A Dog's Love

The fruit of the Spirit is love, joy, peace, patience, kindness, goodness, faithfulness ...

Galatians 5:22

A little boy once prayed, "God, help me to be the kind of person my dog thinks I am." Dogs are so loyal. They forgive you for leaving them behind when you go out. They're always happy to see you. They want to spend all their time with you. Loyalty is a lot like faithfulness.

A girl who has God's Holy Spirit living in her is identifiable by her faithfulness to God ... all the time. It's easy to be faithful to God when you're with other Christians. Then you can say, "Yeah, I love God and I want to obey Him." But how faithful are you when you're with friends who don't care about God? Are you identifiable by your faithfulness to God?

Dear God, it is hard to talk about You and do stuff like pray before lunch when I'm with friends who don't know You. Help me to be more faithful. Amen.

Gentle Me

The fruit of the Spirit is love, joy, peace, patience, kindness, goodness, faithfulness, gentleness ...

Galatians 5:22-23

Some things in life require gentleness. Things like holding a newborn baby, moving your mom's favorite lamp, eggs, other people's feelings. Wait a minute, what was that last one? Yes, it's true.

A girl who has God's Spirit living in her will be identifiable by her gentleness. That means being careful of others' feelings, expressing your ideas and opinions in a kind and gentle way. It can be so easy to jump on the bandwagon of being loud, sarcastic and pushy when your friends are riding that wagon.

Remember, you have God's Spirit living in you and gentleness is His style.

Dear Father, gentleness doesn't come naturally to me. Please help me to be gentle with others so they can see Your love in me. Amen.

Keeping Control

The fruit of the Spirit is love, joy, peace, patience, kindness, goodness, faithfulness, gentleness and self-control.

Galatians 5:22-23

Self-control is important in many different areas of our lives. Take your temper, for example. When you get angry at your little brother and you want to pound him, you have to use self-control to keep your temper from taking over. How about when your mom bakes cookies?

You could eat a plateful if you let yourself. Self-control means you eat only one. Or, when some of your friends are ripping up another girl for her clothes, hair, looks or whatever? You could join in the mean conversation, but self-control stops you. Self-control means that sometimes you don't do or say what you're thinking. A child of God is identifiable by her self-control.

Dear God, okay ... I can't do this one alone 'cause there's too many places where I need self-control. Give me Your strength so I can have self-control. Amen.

Keep the Peace

Remind the people to be subject
to rulers and authorities.

Titus 3:1

Obeying is something you will never outgrow. Well, that sounds depressing, doesn't it? Keep your crown on, Queenie, and listen to this: No matter how grown up you get, there will still be policemen, judges, doctors and others who need to be obeyed.

A well known characteristic of a child of God is obedience – without complaining or fighting. God placed leaders, rulers and teachers in their positions, and they must be respected. It wouldn't look good for a town, nation or country to be torn apart by Christians who resist obeying the leaders of the land. Even if the rulers don't honor God – it's His job to deal with them.

Dear God, I can see how this verse trickles down to people like teachers. Some of my teachers are not easy to be subject to. But I want Your Spirit to shine through me, so please help me to obey. Amen.

Choose God This Day

Set your minds on things above,
not on earthly things.

Colossians 3:2

Every day of your life you set your priorities. You choose how to spend your time, whether to be kind, how to talk about your parents and whether or not to do your homework. You decide if talking on the phone with a friend is more important than prayer time. You choose whether to hang out at the mall or go to youth group at church. You decide what is important to you.

This verse encourages you to look at the big picture; to see what is important in more than just this minute. Because you will grow up, your friends will change, your tastes will change, but the one thing that won't change is God. Make Him your number one priority now.

Dear Father, help me to choose You over all the other things that yell for my attention and loyalty. I want You to be my number one priority. Amen.

Awesome Love

What does the LORD your God ask of you but to fear the LORD your God, to walk in all His ways, to love Him, to serve the LORD your God with all your heart, and with all your soul, and to observe the LORD's commands and decrees.

Deuteronomy 10:12-13

Everything inside you should be straining toward being a girl whose life and character reflect who God is. God doesn't want some of your love and obedience. He isn't interested in your worship on Sunday morning if you ignore Him for the rest of the week.

Read this entire verse – God wants your love and service to come from *all* your heart and *all* your soul. This isn't because He's on a power trip, it's because that's how much He loves you … *completely*.

Dear God, I never thought of it that way before – You want all my love because You give me all of Your love. That's awesome. Thank You! Amen.

A Full Life

"Seek first His kingdom and His righteousness, and all these things will be given to you as well."

Matthew 6:33

You can't outgive God. That's the cool thing about living your life for Him. You don't have to feel like you're giving something up to serve God. The only thing you'll be looking at in your rearview mirror is selfishness, unkindness, loneliness ... sin.

See, some people will tell you that being a Christian takes the fun stuff out of your life. But Jesus said that obeying Him, learning about Him, and serving Him will actually add success, happiness and joy to your life. Sounds like a good deal, doesn't it?

Dear God, help me understand this 'cause some of my friends tell me that serving You takes all the fun out of life. I want to be able to explain how it's totally the opposite. Amen.

Praise Always

Sing joyfully to the LORD, you righteous;
it is fitting for the upright to praise Him.

Psalm 33:1

Do you get it? God loves you so very much. He shows His love every day by taking care of you, providing for your needs, listening to your prayers. He sent Jesus, His only Son, to die for your sins, raised Him back to life, and now He's in heaven getting a place ready for you to spend eternity.

Wow! This deserves your total praise, doesn't it? Sing your praises, shout them, whisper them ... just do it. It gives Him joy to hear your praises and it gives you joy to give them. It's the right thing to do!

Dear Lord, sometimes praise just spills out of me and I want to be comfortable with that happening more and more. I'm so thankful for all You do for me! Amen.

Prayer Time

"Call to Me and I will answer you and tell you great and unsearchable things you do not know."

Jeremiah 33:3

Prayer should be a top priority in your life. It isn't easy, though, to be consistent in your prayer life, is it? You might concentrate on giving a lot of time to prayer for a while, then life gets busy and your prayer time gets pushed aside or compressed to less and less time. What was top priority at first slowly gets pushed down to the bottom priority.

What's amazing is that God offers you so much – if you will just call to Him. Many of His children don't take advantage of that.

He promises to help you understand things you could never dream or imagine if you will just come to Him.

Dear God, I know I'm missing a lot by not talking to You more. I'm sorry – I don't want to hurt You or to miss things in my life. Help me make prayer the top priority in my life. Amen.

God Is Love

"As the Father has loved Me,
so have I loved you."

John 15:9

Jesus spoke these words. Don't read them lightly – think about them. God, the Father, loved His only Son, Jesus, totally and completely. Jesus loves you with that same kind of love. His love doesn't hold back anything, He would do anything for you, in fact He did – He died for you.

When you understand that someone loves you that much, it can change your life. His love for you flows from His Father and fills you. He desires your love in return and your obedience to Him. He also desires that His love for you would cause you to love those around you.

God's love is given to you freely, but is expected to be shared with others.

Dear God, everything about You is love. Please let everything about me be love, too. Amen.

Hurry to Obedience

I will hasten and not delay
to obey Your commands.

Psalm 119:60

"In a minute!" Is that a pretty standard response for just about anything your mom or dad asks you to do? It kind of puts you in control when they ask you to clean your room or load the dishwasher or do your homework, doesn't it? You get to operate on your time frame.

Do you do the same thing with God? "I'll obey You, God, and change the way I live ... in a minute." Yeah, after all, you don't want to miss anything fun by being too spiritual, right? Well, it shouldn't work that way. God doesn't give His love and care to you "in a minute."

Make a choice today to hurry to obey His commands. Make obedience a top priority.

Dear Father, okay, I know I'm guilty of putting off some things that I should be obeying. Please help me to hurry to obedience. Amen.

Unity and Peace

Let the peace of Christ rule in your hearts,
since as members of one body you were called to peace.

Colossians 3:15

Getting along with one another is important. It's important enough that God mentions it in the Bible several times. His children should be different from the rest of the world because of their love for one another.

Little differences that can so easily blow up into big arguments and should be handled right away. All of the "she said this and she did that" stuff that becomes fuel for fire when you whisper about it with other friends ... must stop. Unity and peace are more important.

If you have a problem with someone, go to her alone and talk it out. You'll be glad you did.

Dear Father, it's so easy to just complain to another friend when someone makes me mad. Help me remember to go right to the problem and deal with it so unity and peace aren't ruined. Amen.

God's Gift

"Whoever believes in Him is not condemned, but whoever does not believe stands condemned already because he has not believed in the name of God's one and only Son."

John 3:18

God loves you and wants you to be with Him in heaven forever! That couldn't happen without His gift of Jesus. Way back in the beginning Adam and Eve set sin in motion by choosing to disobey God and that has given people a choice of obeying God or sinning ever since.

God won't allow sinful beings to come into His heaven so He offered a way for us to be cleaned. Jesus took our sins on Himself – died for them – so we don't have to.

So, by choosing to accept Jesus into your heart, repenting or turning away from your sins, and desiring to obey God, you are no longer condemned to stay outside of heaven. Choose Him.

Dear God, I choose Jesus. Thank You for Your gift of love. Amen.

Love Your Enemies

"Love your enemies, do good to those who hate you."

Luke 6:27

Does this verse make you want to shout: "Hey ... you wouldn't say that if you knew my enemies! They're creeps and all they want to do is make my life miserable!" So what? Jesus spent time on this earth teaching people how to live together in unity and peace. He taught that His children should be different from the rest of the world.

If you just love your friends, that's no different from the rest of the world.

If you can be kind and loving to those who aren't kind to you ... that shows God's love.

Suck it up ... don't always just look out for yourself, but show God's love to those who aren't loving to you.

Dear God, You know how hard this is for me. You're gonna have to help me with this ... I want Your help, please. Amen.